First published in 2019 by D&B Publishing

British Library Cataloguing-in-Publication Data
A catalogue record for this book is available from the British Library.

ISBN: 978 1 909457 95 9

Cover by Horacio Monteverde.

Printed and bound in Estonia by Tallinna Raamatutrükikoda.

All sales enquiries should be directed to D&B Poker:
info@dandbpoker.com

www.dandbpoker.com

A Girl's Guide to Poker

BY

AMANDA BOTFELD

Contents

Strategy

Welcome to the Real World

Acknowledgements

First and foremost, I would like to thank all my teachers for believing in me as a writer (and granting leeway for the times I didn't do my homework!) My fourth-grade teacher told me I broke her class record for writing the most pages in the end-of-year writing exam. Fifteen years later, my college professor said the same thing. Teachers like these made me realize I was born to be a writer. I'm incredibly grateful to the California public school system and the University of California, Santa Cruz for its world-class educators.

Discovering poker has been a wild journey; it wasn't always easy. I'd like to thank my friends for hanging with me every step of the way. Their faith never faltered. Speaking of tremendous loyalty, thank you to my boyfriend – whom I met at a poker table – for embracing the losses alongside the wins. The first night we met, he told me: "There are more important things in life than poker." What a pick-up line! He helped me edit and revise this book in romantic language.

Thank you to my fitness trainer for motivating me to write and run. Most of these chapters were written after brutal brainstorming sessions on the treadmill.

Thank you to my publishers for encouraging me to write this book in my own style. And big thanks to my late night proofreader Megan for getting it just it right.

Lastly, thank you to my parents and grandfather. They stand for integrity and making your own luck. They've supported me in all my writing, with my mom always reminding me to "keep it simple." She's my original editor. I would've never started playing poker if it weren't for my dad. He taught me everything I know, including his favorite saying, "Life's a poker game."

P.S. Big thanks to my little brother, Michael. Sorry for all the nonstop poker jargon!

Foreword

The idea behind *A Girl's Guide to Poker* was originally a 45-minute how-to guide I'd mostly written on a plane.

I'd never published a book before, nor was I a famous millionaire poker star. But I knew an easy-to-read beginner's poker book was something that had to be written. I had confidence in my convictions – which, in my experience, can be pretty powerful.

A friend of mine who wrote for *Cardplayer* magazine suggested I research who publishes the poker books I already own and send them an email. I looked up two gaming book publishers, picked the most important-sounding people on their staff, and cold-called them in the form of an email.

They both got back to me. They both wanted it.

As a full-length book.

One publisher sent me comments and notes on the entire manuscript, including approving nods to my *Legally Blonde* references. Who would've thunk a guy who spends his days immersed in gambling was a fan of the great Elle Woods?

But nothing compared to the feedback I received at D&B Poker. Once the sincere and ever-cheery Byron Jacobs at D&B coined me as the "Bridget Jones of Poker," I knew they were the one. Not to mention they are the world's leading poker book publisher. Type in "poker book" on Amazon, and you'll get D&B.

Funny enough, I never set out to write a "women's" poker book. I simply wrote it in my own voice.

When I was in high school art class, we had to showcase our final portfolios. Mine didn't have any particular theme other than getting turned in on time. But I'll never forget what my art teacher had to say, "You can tell that every one of these pieces was made by a woman."

Her comment completely caught me by surprise. Adding a feminine tone or touch had never crossed my mind; I was just trying to paint a picture. I was so struck by the realization it was as though she had uncovered a hidden destiny. I now knew what I wanted to create in the world: art that could say anything about everything in life – proudly said from a female point-of-view.

About the Author

When I was in second-grade, my dad gave me a clunky, grey, calculator-looking handheld video poker device. I brought it to school and played until the batteries died.

That was basically the extent of my poker experience.

The game taught me what-beats-what *(five diamonds is better than 2, 3, 4, 5, 6 in a row)*, and I'd practice for play money with my dad, little brother, and grandfather on holidays like New Year's Eve. That was about it. I never played for real money, and I never played online or with friends. The only person I knew who really liked poker was my dad – and he *really* liked it. His nightstand was filled with poker books. His birthday parties had poker posters[1]. He worked out watching poker replays. My mother even surprised him with a round family poker table that was a regular feature of many family occasions.

Flash forward to age twenty-four. My roommate, Tom, invited me with him to check out the brand new MGM casino right outside Washington D.C. – I couldn't wait! I thought was going to be a poker superstar just like my dad.

Instead I got crushed. Oops!

I didn't even know the basics. *The level of poker I'd been playing was for kids.* I knew some stuff, but not nearly enough. Video poker taught me that two pair beats one pair, but not that two pair can get "counterfeited." Or that a full house can lose to a bigger full house. Or how to bet-size. All of a sudden I wished I would've payed more attention to my dad's TV shows.

At the time, I was working three blocks away from The White House as a nerdy "research associate," and tried to learn poker by the only

---

1 Granted it's really hard to plan birthdays for guys, so I'm pretty sure that's why we always went with poker theme.

way I knew how: reading a book. I must've called every bookstore in D.C. – they all acted like I was crazy. They were more likely to have books on Ho Chi Minh than Hold 'Em. Eventually I took an Uber car 45 minutes away to a Barnes & Nobles in a strip mall in Virginia – the only place I could find with books on poker. They had two.

Talk About Clueless!

"You played that hand horribly," a man told me once. I asked him how so. "Well for starters," he replied, "I could see your cards."

The books were way too hard for me to understand. My background was in Israeli-Palestinian relations, and these were denser than anything I'd ever read. It was easier for me to dissect articles on Iran's Intercontinental Ballistic Missile program than "fold equity" jargon.

The few times I tried playing poker again was a (very expensive) disaster. I wish I could say I was learning the hard way, but I wouldn't even go that far. I wasn't getting any better. More poker didn't make me more profitable. My roommate Tom already had all these poker probabilities memorized – numbers which were completely bewildering to me. I was never good at math and flunked eighth-grade algebra. The whole experience made me feel like a loser, an assessment confirmed by my wallet.

The breakthrough happened when I found a miraculous chart on the internet. The chart stated *exactly* which cards to play and was a standard "pre-flop raise chart" like the one found in page 70. I converted it into cute color-coded flashcards labeled with stickers. There were more than 180 flashcards in total, and I studied them on my lunch breaks.

Poker became a different game. Most of the time I just folded by instruction of my holy chart, but the hands I did play, I won. The math started to make more sense. I joined a kickball league mostly made up of poker dealers, and they'd drill me on "find the winning hand" at the after-game bar parties. I met poker friends and poker coaches. I input all my hands into a free poker calculator app on my phone[2]. That way I knew if I did the right thing or had just gotten lucky.

By the time I entered my first tournament three months later, I won first place. Six months later I was the seventh-highest ranked tournament player at the MGM National Harbor casino in Maryland. Two months after that I was sitting at a table next to the man who had won the 2015 World Series of Poker Main Event (the biggest competition in poker) in a $3,000 entry fee tournament, a seat I earned by winning a less expensive "satellite" tournament – twice.

Less than a year into my poker career, I had gone from someone who didn't know how to hold her cards right to bumping elbows with the guys my dad watched on TV.

My main job as a political writer was to create a daily newsletter for 30,000 subscribers about what was going on in Israel and across the Middle East. Letting people know the most important information in a few quick and simple sentences. What was on a "need-to-know" basis. The bottom lines. The bullet points. I decided to do the same with this book except instead of politics made simple, poker made simple.

2 Check out the Know the Odds trainer on my website amandasaces.com

I hope you learn as much reading it as I did writing it.

Your Friend on the Felt, **Amanda**

Introduction

There are more ways to shuffle a card deck than there are atoms on Earth (80,000,000,000,000,000,000,000,000,000,000,000, 000,000,000,000,000,000,000,000,000,000,000 combos, to be exact). And almost as many poker books have been written.

This book is different.

It's not your high school math textbook, and it's certainly not your dad's old school Texas Hold'em guide. It's fun. It's simple. It's quick! It's poker made easy, a poker book for people who don't play poker. Told with female flair and girlish glam, *A Girl's Guide to Poker* teaches the ins and outs of the game with style, sophistication, and moxie.

No woman has ever won the World Series of Poker Main Event, even though first prize is several million dollars and a glitzy diamond bracelet. Ninety-five per cent of the competitors are men (why they'd want a $50,000 bracelet, I will never know). That's because seeing women at poker tables is like flopping a set or making or a flush[1] – it happens, but don't count on it.

This book aims to make that change.

Before You Read This Book

Be aware that people spend their entire lives studying poker. They hire coaches, listen to podcasts, watch videos, read magazines – the list goes on. A professional poker player I know writes 5-page essays analyzing individual poker hands (he keeps them in a blue binder with nice little sticky tabs). For some, starting to learn poker is just cards. For others, it's opening Pandora's box.

There are also portions in *A Girl's Guide to Poker* dedicated to poker fun stuff. Crazy cash game stories. Poker on the brain. Gambling trivia. Expand your game into body language and psychology. In

---

1 Don't worry if you don't catch all the poker jargon (yet!).

writing this book, I spoke with a former FBI secret service agent, a gambling historian, and a poker psychotherapist. Poker is a series of moving parts. *If you*  *play long enough, you will either witness or experience every emotion on the spectrum of human imagination.*

Poker digs into the deepest parts of the human psyche, and is played by doctors, lawyers, and construction workers. The highest-ranked female poker player in the world[2] graduated from Yale law school and works for a Wall Street hedge fund. Sam Trickett, one of the greatest (and richest[3]) poker players of all time, used to be a plumber. Go figure.

You may have heard the expression "there is more to life than..." There is more to life than money. There is more to life than marriage. There is more to life than fill-in-the-blank.

Consider this reversal by Tom McEvoy, four-time World Series of Poker bracelet-winner and member of the Poker Hall of Fame: "There is more to poker than life."

By the end of this book, you'll know what that means.

Every poker player does.

---

2 Vanessa Selbst.

3 He has more than $20 million in live earnings and is #18 on the poker All Time Money List.

A Women's Poker Book

When I first spoke to a female a poker pro about writing *A Girl's Guide to Poker*, she liked the idea, but wanted to make sure it wasn't... well... stupid. (I believe her word was "diminutive").

"Like pink razors?" I replied.

"Exactly", she said.

Not that anything is wrong with pink razors *in theory*, but anyone who has ever used a standard drug-store pink blade knows they are dull, cheap, and low quality. *A Girl's Guide* needed to be different.

Feminine, but also sharp.

A Girl's Guide to Poker is clearly told in a woman's voice. It's fun. It's flirty. It's upbeat. It's unapologetically female in style – *not in substance*. The content is just as hefty as any traditional man's poker book. Because female doesn't mean "lite".

Fewer women play poker, and for many reasons. Casinos are a boys' club, practicing poker online is anti-social, girls aren't encouraged

> **A Girl's Guide to Poker may have a silly style but it has smart advice.**

to be as competitive and so on. I'd say the main reason, however, is that the game isn't inclusive to beginners.

You can't learn poker overnight.

Learning poker is like learning a language – it takes everyday practice. And whereas guys have frat parties and camping trips and military missions and beer games to practice gradually, casually, and safely, I've never had a girlfriend invite me to a poker game. Ever.

Most men and women who play poker learned from someone else. And if you weren't in groups who played poker, you were basically S.O.L.[1]

The idea behind *A Girl's Guide* was to make poker friendly. This book is the cool, chic, poker-playing friend you've always wanted.

And she tells pretty good jokes too.

---

1 Sh–t out of luck.

What Do You Mean "Poker"?

There are two types of poker: No-Limit Texas Hold'em, and everything else. NLHE is the game you see on most TV shows and casino poker tables. When someone says they're going to play poker, they almost always mean No-Limit Texas Hold'em - unless they are over the age of 65. Then it's anybody's guess.

Dating back to around 20 B.C. (before computers), very few people even knew how to play Texas Hold'em. Let alone "No-Limit" style.

They played seven-card stud, five-card draw, and most likely six-card something or other. When they finally discovered the beauty of Texas Hold'em, they played with limits, capping the bets so you can't win or lose too much. Grandpa poker.

No-Limit Texas Hold'em is more aggressive. More risky. And more popular (because no one ever got cool by being square!) It is also the subject of this book.

When I Say Poker, I Mean No-Limit Texas Hold'em

Card rooms and casinos are a collection of NLHE, with a few Limit tables for the old school veterans. Maybe even seven-card stud for the true salts of the earth. You'll also find one or two Omaha and mixed game tables - new games for the young guns. These are twists on Texas Hold'em which make the game more complex and add a little more gamble. The poker evolution continues.

But before you go running to purchase the hot new master class on Short-Deck poker or Badugi, just know that these newer variations are highly specialized and avant-garde – they're not for everyone.

The Sky's the Limit!
Limit poker caps how much you can bet.
No Limit poker means there is no max!

They don't have the same universal "anyone-can-play" vibe as Texas Hold 'Em. They're niche.

That's why as poker trends come and go, NLHE will always be in style. It's the Maybelline mascara, the wear-with-anything jeans, the classic white tee. Dressed up or down, the game is here to stay.

Call it a wardrobe staple.

Or a carry-on must-have.

Or simply the greatest game ever.

PRO TIP

Poker strategy transformed from making the right decision in any given moment to *making the right decision over time.*

Poker's Makeover: From Doyle to Doug

Poker is almost unrecognizable from how it was played just a few years ago. Call the modern makeover From Doyle to Doug – the double-D's of poker.

Doyle Brunson is nicknamed "the Godfather of Poker," an old school Texas cowboy who helped start the World Series of Poker and wrote the big bible on Hold'em. He published *How I Made Over $1,000,000 Playing Poker* (title changed to *Super System*) in 1978 back when a dozen eggs cost $0.82. He introduced the world to Texas Hold 'Em and demonstrated how to hold a poker face on TV. "Show me your eyes and you may as well show me your cards," said Doyle.

Compare that to a quote from one of the most influential figures in poker today: "I never go with my instincts. I do what I think makes most sense," the 29-year-old fast-talking, bro-tank-wearing, multimillionaire poker celeb Doug Polk said on YouTube in 2018. He was livestreaming a bankroll challenge during which he turned $100 into $10,000. Many of his decisions were determined by a calculator.

Doyle tried to interpret specific situations accurately. The old way was about winning that one time, but the new way is about winning 100x.

Play the percentages.

Luck or Skill?

Is poker a game of luck or skill? It is 100%, undoubtedly, without question a game of skill - *after a certain point.*

An amateur can beat a pro in any one random poker hand easily. There are plenty of clips featuring clueless rookies winning against seasoned millionaire professionals; I'd bet right now that even if you have zero experience, you'd be able to win a few hands too. Short-term Texas Hold'em comes down to the luck of the draw, and there's a saying in poker "better to be lucky than good."

But luck always runs out. Only solid players can consistently beat the game.

When does luck become eclipsed by skill?

At just under 1,500 hands. 1,471 to be exact. Glad you asked.

1,471 is usually between 19 and 25 hours. Less if you're multi-tabling online (way less[1]). Elite players predictably perform better according to researchers[2]. Investors, take note:

- ♦ Those ranked in the top 10% in the first six months of the year were more than twice as likely to do similarly well in the next six months.

- ♦ Players who finished in the best-performing 1% in the first half of the year were 12 times more likely than others to repeat the feat in the second half.

- ♦ Players who fared badly from the start continued to lose.

As my grandmother used to say, the cream always rises to the top!

---

1 Online tables are 3x faster than live (100+ hands/hr vs 30 hands/hr). Multiply that by how many tables you're playing and you've entered hyperspeed.
2 *Study: Beyond Chance? The Persistence of Performance in Online Poker*, Rogier J. D. Potter van Loon et al. Published March 2, 2015.

Here's Why

A 103 million-hand online poker study by Citigal, Inc., in conjuction with PokerStars, revealed two important conclusions:

♦ Three-quarters of all hands never go to showdown .

♦ Only about 12% of hands are won by who has the best cards.

Most of the time the winner doesn't even have the best hand! This means the good players win by *outplaying* their opponents rather than *outdrawing* them. Poker may seem like a crazy gambling scheme, but there is a method to the madness.

The results of a 103 million-hand study determined that Texas Hold'em is 88% skill.

Think of it like the lottery. Let's say you risk $1.00 to win $1,000,000. You *know* most of the time you aren't going to win. But the payoff is big enough for you to gamble your buck to win a million.

Poker Brain Science

An apple a day keeps the doctor away, but if the doctor is cute, forget the fruit.

Dr. Tricia Cardner has two PhDs – psychology and criminology – plus major game. She is a psychology consultant who specializes in peak poker performance[1]. It's not just cards. It's brain science.

♦ **Mind Push-Ups:** Poker strengthens the brain and protects nerve cells.

♦ **Brain Game:** Recent studies show that playing poker can reduce your chances of developing brain-related diseases like Alzheimer's by as much as 50%.

Poker Psychology

1) The brain reacts emotionally before logically.

2) The pain of losing money is greater than the pleasure of winning money.

I'm Not a Scientist!

My expertise in biology extends to clicking random YouTube videos with titles such as *Why You Should Never Swallow Gum*, *What If You Only Drank Coffee And Nothing Else?* and *Do Plants Think?* Sometimes I'll even read a magazine article solving which waist-to-hip ratio is most attractive. Or Google if my dog knows he's cute.[2]

So when it came to poker science, I decided to phone a friend. Fortunately, Dr. Tricia was there to save the day, and answered all my questions about "Poker on the Mind." (the name of Tricia's podcast).

---

1 Buy her books: *Peak Poker Performance*, *Positive Poker*, and *Purposeful Practice for Poker* (dandbpoker.com).
2 He totally does.

Feel First, Think Later

When processing information, "we have an emotional reaction almost instantaneously," Dr. Tricia says. "Before we ever even stop and think rationally." We intake through our senses - what we see, hear, and feel. The "first stop on the train tracks" after travelling up the brain stem is feelings, feelings, feelings. (Does "gut instinct" really mean "limbic system" instinct?) Then it travels onto the logic centers of the brain - planning, reasoning, and decision-making.

This is why Dr. Tricia thinks women could truly excel in poker.

We need to learn how to process our feelings if we want to think straight.

Learn Poker the Smart Way

PRO TIP

Girl after my own heart! I learned poker very quickly by making cute color-coded flashcards with stickers.

Let's say you want to start playing No-Limit Hold'em ASAP. *What's the fastest way to learn poker?* Is it better to play a bunch of hands to get familiar, or do drills?

"It's 100% better to do the drills,"

... says Dr. Tricia.

Dr. Tricia prescribes flashcards, videos, and online poker trainers (you can try mine on my website amandasaces.com). "I can do 10,000 hours but if my practice is not quality, then nothing is going to happen," explains the doctor. She points to her co-writer Jonathan Little who *deposited $50 online and quickly turned it into $300,000 - but had spent six months prior studying without playing a single hand.*

Less is More

Poker is *not* like running. You run every day, you're going to get faster. But you could play poker every day and remain a slowpoke.

Easily.

- ♦ Playing more poker doesn't mean playing better poker.
- ♦ A little poker each day will accelerate you faster than a chunk 1x/week.

Easy, Now!

For our minds, learning a new skill is "circuit-training" (mental work-out time!) "The first time you fire the circuit, it doesn't go very fast. The message goes slow because you don't really know what you're doing," explains Dr. Tricia. "But the more you fire that circuit, the faster the messages travel."

The neurons get *myelinated* in the brain. "Myelination is like insulation; whenever you fire a neural circuit, a tiny bit of myelin wraps around the neuron. The more myelin you build up, the more insulated the circuit becomes and the faster the neuron is going to fire."

Basically, it gets better. **Faster. Easier. Simpler**. Like learning to drive a car - at first you don't know on which pedals to place your feet, and later you're talking, chewing, and listening to the radio. Slow down, sister!

Do I Have to be Smart to Play Poker?

"When we're testing people in the U.S.A., we're usually looking at working memory-based intelligence [IQ tests]," explains Dr. Tricia. "But there are many types of intelligences. Maybe you didn't do that great in school. That doesn't mean you don't have a lot of social and/or emotional intelligence." She even suggests that certain professional poker players with a very high IQ would improve their results if they worked on their people skills.

PRO TIP

"This thing called 'intelligence' only accounts for maybe 20% of the variance in success generally speaking," says Dr. Tricia, a woman who is clearly good at doing homework. "Yes, you need to have a certain understanding of math and logic to learn poker. *But it's not rocket science.*"

Tell Me a Story

The key to good poker is storytelling.

When you wager a large amount of money, you are telling the story you have a premium hand – bluffers should steer clear! Investing the bare minimum says your cards aren't that great.

You will hear phrases such as "the story doesn't add up" or "her story doesn't make sense" all the time from poker commentators (No, I didn't just say the crux of poker is storytelling because I'm a writer - it's a known poker terminology!) Telling a coherent story is how you play the game instead of how you play your cards.

The last golden age of American women as storytellers was old Hollywood (unless you count the MySpace-Facebook-Tumblr blogger explosion). Half of all films copyrighted between 1911 and 1925 were written by women – even *Gentleman Prefer Blondes*, the iconic Marilyn Monroe classic, was adapted from a book written by Ms. Anita Loos in the 1920s. Lights! Camera! Suffrage![1]

While poker is very math-oriented and utilizes skills that are traditionally "guyish," creative, connected, right-brain thinking is a major asset.

> **Make the Story Fabulous!**
> Whenever you're playing poker, ask yourself what story you're telling.

---

1 Important moment in history: the women's suffrage movement secured women's right to vote in 1920.

Bad poker players try to win by force. They aren't in touch with the other players at the table, and think jamming chips into oblivion counts as good strategy. An inflexible style won't goad your opponents into bending to your will. And that's what makes a poker player brilliant: getting people to do what they want. Learn people, learn poker.

The more in tune you are with your opponent's way of thinking, the more successful you will be as a player.

And as a person.

♣ ♣ Quiz Level One: Clubs ♣ ♣

Keep track of your answers. Correct answers score 10 points!

1) What is the biggest tournament in poker?

a) The Spades Cup.

b) The Main Event.

c) Wimblebluff.

d) Deuces Cracked.

2) In addition to prize money, the winner receives a ...

a) Car.

b) Bracelet.

c) Belt buckle.

d) Diamond-studded card protector.

3) True or False: Poker is the same as it was 15 years ago.

a) True.

b) False.

c) EXTREMELY false!

4) When does skill overcome luck?

a) Trick question, skill always beats luck.

b) Poker is all luck. The only skill is leaving!

c) Around playing 500 hands.

d) Around playing 1,500 hands.

Bonus points for the exact number! _____

5) Finish this poker saying! "It's better to be ___ than good"

a) Great.

b) Bad.

c) Dangerous.

d) Lucky.

6) True or False: The brain reacts emotionally before rationally.

a) True.

b) False.

c) *My emotions are rational!!!*

7) Will you learn poker faster by playing or studying?

a) Playing – this study quiz is boring me already.

b) Sexy nerdy studying.

8) The key to playing poker is...

a) Making a good bluff.

b) Catching a bad bluff.

c) Keeping a stone poker face.

d) Telling a good story.

WORD SEARCH

```
D B V F Y O B R A C E L E T P J R C C T
O L W T J V U Q U P E I Y S E O P J C H
Y U P A N D O R A L I D O W S B K X B I
L F N B Y E M O T I O N S Z I S U E G N
E F D G S T O R Y T E L L E R R Z V R K
```

Answers on page 202.

Where to Start

The most important part of poker is not learning how to play. It's *where* to play.

Hands down.

Many people could easily transform themselves into winning players if they only knew how to choose the right poker game. And you might be surprised to find that some of the lowest stakes games are actually the hardest to beat.

Poker is a lot like life - try not to shoot yourself in the foot! Don't swig shots before a test. Don't karaoke Eminem. Don't start a diet on your birthday. Whether you're after weight loss or wallet gain, set yourself up for success.

PRO TIP

The table you sit down at will directly impact how much you win or lose.

Giving yourself an edge comes down to *game selection*.

Game Selection Deal-Breaker #1: Price to Play

Life isn't fair, so we create games with rules that give everyone an equal opportunity to win. But poker isn't communism. Instead of *winning* equally, poker requires *paying* equally - everyone must spend! (Take that, Stalin) Spending the *absolute minimum* to play a single poker hand is called paying the blinds.

Everyone at a poker table takes turns going first. And everyone at the table takes turns paying the blinds - *whether they want to or not.* You could be given good cards. You could be given bad cards. Doesn't matter. When it's your turn to pay the blinds, you don't even need to see your cards - you could be wearing a blindfold! Thus the name **blinds**. Get it? It's short for blind bet, since you have to pay without looking.

Blinds are written like this: $1/$2, $5/$10, $100/$200, and the list goes on. You will also come across $2/$5 or $3/$5, because no one carries coins anymore. Los Angeles is known for $5/$5 games since Hollywood celebrities are turned off by anything normal, whether it's baby names or poker games.

Blinds *anchor* the amount it costs for anyone to play. The bigger the big blind, the bigger the minimum price. If a friend invites you to a $1/$2 game, expect to spend *at least* $2 whenever you want to play a hand. Every. single. time. If a friend invites you to a $100/$200 game, forget about poker and ask them to buy you a trip to France.

Blinds sound more complicated than they are - most people get the hang of them in less than 10 minutes of playing.

Now for a major secret...

Blinds reveal a game's **Luck Factor**.

Poker is a game of skill. Better players win more often, which is why the same few guys are always winning poker tournaments on TV. "If it weren't for luck, I'd win every time," says Phil Hellmuth, famous for being one of the best poker players of all time, and also for having one of the world's biggest egos.

But some poker games have more luck by design.

To determine a game's luck factor, calculate the MAX number of big blinds you can buy in for. A $1/$2 game with a $200 max allows up to 100 big blinds (200/2). A $1/$2 game with a $100 max allows up to 50 big blinds (100/2).

Let's say a game doesn't let you buy in for more than $20, and the blinds are $5/$10. That means you only have TWO big blinds before losing all your money! You're going to be risking all your chips all the time. Ouch. It's a forced gamble. Since you can't outplay your opponents with so few chips, you're going to have to be dealt better cards than them. A typical $5/$10 game will have people buying in for $1,000 or more, spending $10 at the get-go, and then increasing the price of play throughout the hand. This allows them to pull big bluffs and maximize their skill.

PRO TIP

Games with less than 50 big blinds are **luckfests**. Silver lining: games with few big blinds are more luck-based than skill-based, meaning amateurs have a fairer shot against pros.

Anything under 20 big blinds is playing *Bingo!* Games with $1/$2 blinds and a max buy-in of $100 are crazier than five-year-old Youtubers. They are trouble!

Game Selection Deal-Breaker #2: Competition

Two poker players are lost in the wilderness. A bear jumps out of the bushes and starts chasing them. They're about to start running, but one stops to tie her shoes.

Her friend says, "What are you doing? You can't outrun a bear!"

The other friend replies, "I don't have to outrun the bear. I only have to outrun you!"

Ha-ha! So is life.

Moral of the story: you can be the 10th best poker player in the world, but if you're playing against the top nine, you're likely going to lose. DON'T pick on someone your own size!

Steer clear of tables where everyone is wearing sunglasses and headphones – these are not newbies. Also look out for players watching poker games on their smartphones. Yes, it does happen! Some people would have cards injected into them in IV fluid if they could. Find casual, chatty, easygoing games where chips aren't stacked into neat little piles. Forget what your roommate said: *Messy is good.* Slop-py. Scattered. Disor-ganized. Most regular poker players know exactly how they like to organize their chips. Many maintain nice little towers. They never have dif-ferent colored poker chips mixed togeth-er – it's a *faux paus* called a dirty stack).

- ◆ The Poker Tournament Directors Association recommends keeping chip stacks in multiples of 20.
- ◆ Always keep your highest-priced chips in front where everyone can see them.
- ◆ Organizing chips into teeny tiny piles looks strange to the trained eye.

WARNING!...

Playing against *terrible* players can be just as challenging as playing against very good players.

You can't understand *complete* beginners because they don't understand the game themselves. They may think they have better cards than they really do. Or the reverse. They will also play extremely unconventional holdings, getting lucky on you with kooky cards. And forget about bluffing – they're too curious! Remember the underlying motivations: pros play to win, beginners play to learn. Amateurs will often call assuming they're losing but just want to see your cards. Lastly, it's impossible to act like you have a straight, flush, or full house against a rookie player because they don't know what those things are. Don't try to outsmart beginners - it won't work!

Game Selection Deal-Breaker #3: House Cut

Poker is the only game where you play against other people rather than the casino. So how is Vegas still in business?

Relax: Vegas will be fine. Your New Year's Eve plans in Sin City aren't on hold. Casinos are extremely profitable - for the house, that is.

Whenever someone wins a hand at a casino, the house takes a cut (and you thought only salespeople earned commissions!). This is the *rake*. Let's say you win $70. The casino might take $7 of it away - without you even noticing. Sneakier than signing your life away before checking "I have read and agree to all the terms and conditions."[1]

Some places charge a higher rake than others. Slot machines are banned in many California casinos, meaning more of their profits

---

1 Or a bad prenup.

come from card games, making the rake higher there than, say, Vegas. Poker profits are a drop in a bucket for Vegas casinos; they tax poker players less.

Online cardrooms don't have to pay as many employees or building expenses, which can also give them more flexibility. Underground games like those you might find in New York are generally the worst: they can charge whatever they want. Plus they absorb the risk of operating illegally. Crime doesn't pay... or does it?

Take a totally typical casino example.

+ You and 10 friends each have $200.

+ Y'all go to a casino and sit down at the same poker table. Because #squadgoals.

+ Blinds are $1/$2 and the average rake taken is $4.

Q) If you played from noon to midnight, how much of your $200 would each of you have left?

A) Zero. The answer is **zero**.

You and your entire crew will have gone broke.

The night out cost $2,000.

And you thought bars were expensive!

Here's how:

+ Dealer deals 30 hands/hour.

+ Every hour the casino takes $120 in rake ($4 rake x 30 hands).

+ The casino takes $30/hour for jackpots ($1 per hand).

+ Tips add up to $30/hour ($1 per hand for the dealer).

+ **Grand total is $180 per hour!**

Twelve hours later your wallets will be empty.

Should I play?

Rake impact is so exaggerated in certain games that winning is an uphill battle. (Especially if people are buying-in for small amounts.)

"Unbeatable" is how poker analyst and owner of Crush Live Poker training site Bart Hanson classifies high-rake, low-stakes games (generally buy-ins of $100 or less).

"I am very confident that those games cannot be beaten by anyone."

He doesn't believe even poker legend Phil Ivey - who has more than 26 million in tournament earnings and is considered one of the greatest poker players of all time - could overcome the casino collection.

That's not to say it's all doom and gloom. Entry-level games even with poor structures have their value: getting experience with handling chips, different player types, and the general pace of play. Plus they can be fun! I know some poker pros who hop into these *Bingo!*-style games for every once in a blue moon. Just know what you're getting into: these games are for recreation rather than profit.

True Story

A friend of mine plays poker online in New Jersey during his free time. Internet cardrooms also take a smaller amount than live casinos because they have fewer business operating costs.

He was pleased with his results for 2017: $3,000 profit. The exact number was $2,814 as tracked by a standard poker software program which also calculated the rake. He paid over **$30,000(!!)** in rake. The true number was $35,801.

If there was no rake, he'd be more than 30 grand richer.

PRO TIP

Remember the three deal breakers:

Blinds, Competition, Rake

If a poker game isn't good to you in these three categories, stand your ground! A bad game is fine for a fling, but you won't be able to build a solid future.

Most games where you can sit down with 100 big blinds have the *Girl's Guide* blessing.

Baby's Gotta Know the Basics

Texas Hold'em has its own **rhythm**.

At first it's hard to follow, and you'll probably feel like you have two left feet. But once you catch the beat, the steps become easy, and you'll be jamming along like a poker-playing pop star.

Order in the Court!

Poker has a very specific order. Because every rhyme needs a little reason.

Step 1
The dealer gives everyone two cards. These are called *hole cards*.

Step 2
Everyone peeks at their cards. Each person is given a choice to keep participating, deciding if they want to play; and, if so, for how much. This round is called *pre-flop*, because it happens before the next round, which is called...

Step 3
... the flop! "Flop" is one of the most important words in poker. This is a term you absolutely need to know. *Flop, flop, flop.* Say it ten times, write it on the back of your hand in thick felt-tip sharpie. Memorize this better than the lyrics to your favorite 90s song.

("Baby, bye! bye! bye!" is "Baby, flop, flop, flop!"[1])

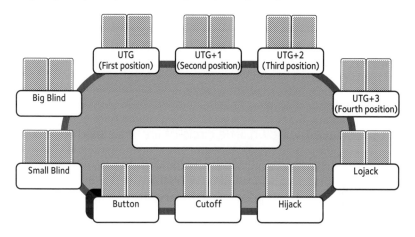

Names and positions at the poker table.

The three flop cards are dealt in the center of the table *face-up*, so everyone can see them.

All the players take a turn reacting to the flop cards by betting, raising, or folding.

Step 4
Next a fourth card is dealt face-up in the center of the table for everyone to see. This is called *the turn*. Once again, everyone reacts by betting, raising, or folding.

Quick and Dirty Version
Everyone gets two secret personal cards, and takes turns deciding if they want to play. Then there are three more rounds (flop, turn, river) with cards dealt publicly for everyone to see. Each round is an opportunity to bet more money.

---

1 "Bye Bye Bye" is a song by American boy band NSYNC, released on January 11, 2000, a hair past the end of the 90s. No disrespect to Justin Timberlake.

Step 5
Lastly a fifth card is dealt face-up, called *the river*. Everyone has one last chance to bet. You win by everyone else folding or turning over the best hand after the round is completed. This final reveal is the great big *showdown*.

Button Up!

Poker tables have their own little circle of life. It's called the **button**.

The button is a small circular object which rotates to the left around the table. Whoever has the button gets to act last - a huge advantage! If you ever want to know Whose ~~Line~~ Turn Is it Anyway? Find the button.

Gameplay order centers around which person at the table has the button.

Button envy? Don't worry – everyone at the table gets a turn to have the button. FOMO[2] unnecessary.

2 Fear of Missing Out. The "Fear of Missing Out" phenomenon was first identified in 1996 by marketing strategist Dr. Dan Herman. It is now listed in the Merriam-Webster and Oxford dictionaries.

How to peek at your cards properly.

Gameplay order stays the same with *one* exception. Before the flop, the player three places to the left of the button acts first. After the flop, the player directly to the left of the button always goes first. This is simpler than it sounds. Poker flow is very intuitive, and here's the best part: it never changes!

Learn it once and you've learned it forever.

Sneak a Peek

People judge books by their covers, and will likely judge you by how you cover your cards.

When you first look at your cards, make sure you do so very carefully – you don't want anyone seeing what you have. *Do not* lift your cards up off the table. Poker is not UNO. Only slightly lift the top of the cards with one hand, and cup your other hand over in a protective cover. This conceals your cards - and shows off your new manicure.

Position is Power!

Lauren Conrad[1] from MTV's *The Hills* was once asked on-radio, "What's your favorite position?"

Her response, "CEO."

Whether in the bedroom, boardroom, or Bellagio cardroom, there is nothing more important than **position**.

You may notice that most poker how-to books start with gameplay moves (what it means to check, bet, raise, or fold), and then explain position. You may also notice that most poker players are losing players.

That's because position is everything *(see the chart in this chapter on page 46 for how position predicts your win rate)*. It's better to choose different cards based on your position at the table, so it makes sense to understand the positions before cards. Trust me, you'll thank me later.

Your position at the table changes which cards you should play.

What do you Mean "Position"?

Everyone takes turns in poker. Sometimes you will be first to act. Sometimes second. Or third. Or fourth. And so on. Wherever you fall in the order is your position. If you are one of the first few people to act, you are in *early position.* Caught in the middle? You are, fittingly, in *middle position.* The last few people to act are in what is called *late position.*

Most poker tables have seats for nine to ten players. Everyone will have a chance to play in all seat positions. Like musical chairs, except less cardio.

---

1 Fifteen years post *The Hills*, Lauren is now a married mum with a handsome lawyer husband. She also became a *New York Times* bestselling author and has an affordable swimwear line at Kohl's.

Why is Position So Important?

Poker is an information game, and your position will give you more clues into what's behind other people's cards. Pay attention, Sherlock!

If you are in late position, you get to see what everyone else does first. Adjust your decisions accordingly.

Late position is best. Early position is worst.

Acting first in one of the early positions is like taking shots in the dark - even a studly American sniper couldn't shoot straight.

Pokerstars – the world's largest poker site – studied different poker hands to see which positions win the most pots. *The last person to act won nearly 50% more times than the person in first position!*

Do nice girls finish last?

That we'll never know, but poker players who act last make more money.

Every position at the poker table has a nickname. Knowing the names is handy, but if you're a total beginner, just keep in mind that *first is worst*[2].

---

2 You can practice learning the names of the positions with my "Take A Seat!" quiz on amandasaces.com.

- **Early positions:** Under the Gun (UTG) acts first, followed by UTG+1, followed by UTG+2.

- **Middle positions:** Middle Position (MP), followed by Hijack.

- **Late positions:** Cutoff (CO), followed by Button.

- **Special positions:** Small Blind (SB), followed by Big Blind (BB). These play a little different because they are last to act pre-flop but first to act from then on. These are bad positions for these reasons and also because you are obliged to commit money to the pot before seeing your cards.

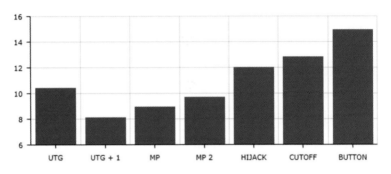

Profit by Position[3]

Here's a Bright Idea

If you are just starting out, consider folding all hands in early positions. *Don't even look!* Your decisions in late positions will be easier since you will have seen what other players did first – and thus speed up the learning curve!

Fly High, Supergirl!

Annette Obrestadt won an online poker tournament *without looking at her cards*. That's right – she beat 179 opponents playing "blind." The 20-something-year-old pro put tape on the computer screen so she couldn't see her cards[4]. Why (and how!) did she do it? In her words, "[to] show just how important it is to play position and to pay attention to the players at the table." Watching other players act first gave her all the information she needed.

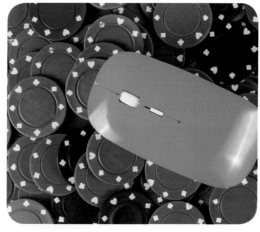

4 Annette posted video of her playing the entire tournament, which is available online for the diehard fans and skeptic non-believers! Nowadays she posts makeup tutorials and reviews on her Youtube channel Annette's Makeup Corner. You glow, girl!

How to Win

Effeuiller la marguerite is a French game where you pick petals off a daisy flower to determine if your crush feels the same way about you, better known as, "He loves me, he loves me not."[1] What a girl wouldn't give for a little clarity.

It's hard to know where you really stand with another person, if you selected the right career path or the right college major (at the right time), or if you truly are "being your best self!" Psychics, tarot cards readers and life coaches make fortunes trying to make people's worlds clearer and more concrete. I'm a big fan of astrology, because I like organizing and classifying people into systems (and my moon sign is also in super nitpicky Virgo[2]). But people aren't boxes, and life is full of competing truths. There isn't always a right answer - except in poker.

"Nothing is black-and-white, except for winning and losing, and maybe that's why people gravitate to that so much," said eight-time NBA All-Star professional basketball player Steve Nash.

---

1 Or "She loves me, she loves me not."
2 I'm a Pisces, Aries rising, Virgo moon. Thanks for asking!

There is something deeply satisfying about winning. On, like, a deep profound human psychological level or something.

Winning in Poker

There are two ways to win in poker: have the best cards, or bluff.

Poker is winner-takes-all.

Does the person with the second-best hand get anything? Nope – don't shoot for leftovers!

The winner scoops all the chips in the center of the table ("the pot.") This is the world's best kind of pot, better than any grass you've ever smoked.

Bluff Your Way to Victory

Winning through bluffing is very simple. When all remaining opponents fold (throw away) their cards, you win by forfeit - without ever having to show your hand. If they give up, victory is yours.

Why would anyone want to fold? On every round (pre-flop, flop, turn, river), staying in the game can get much more expensive. Your opponent may even suspect you are bluffing, but may fold anyways if the price is too high.

- ♦ You win in poker when everyone else folds.
- ♦ Winning by bluffing is extra satisfying because it tests your skill, bravery, and mettle!

Matchmaker, Matchmaker, Make Me a Match!

"Matchmaker, matchmaker, make me a match!" are not only the lyrics to a hit Broadway musical[3], but the theory behind winning in poker using your cards. *You need to make a match.*

3 Fiddler on the Roof, *meshugganah.*

A good match is hard to find! You and the other players will all be trying to couple your own personal hole cards with the community cards. Best pairing wins.

> There are 52 cards in a deck, two more than *50 Shades of Grey*. And there are 2,598,960 combinations of hands by the river.

Certain combinations of cards are better than others. To win at the big reveal (aka showdown), you don't need the best possible card combination, only a better card combination than your opponent(s).

My Hand Beats Your Hand!

At the end there will be a total of seven cards — your two hole cards plus the five community cards. Your final poker hand is the best five card combination using all seven.

1) Royal Flush
Nothing beats a royal flush. This is the best hand (*extremely rare!*) Must specifically be ace, king, queen, jack, 10 all in the same suit.

A♥-K♥-Q♥-J♥-10♥

2) Straight Flush
Five cards in a row in the same suit. Also extremely rare.

3♣-4♣-5♣-6♣-7♣

3) Four-of-a-Kind
Four of the same card. Nicknamed quads. (Completed by the highest remaining card available so your combo still uses five cards out of the seven.)

8♥-8♦-8♣-8♠-A♥

4) Full House
Three-of-a kind with a pair.

9♥-9♦-9♣-K♠-K♥

5) Flush
Any five cards in the same suit.

4♦-6♦-2♦-9♦-A♦

6) Straight
Series of five cards that follow each other.

6♣-7♥-8♣-9♦-10♠

7) Three-of-a-Kind
Any three cards which are the same. (Completed by the highest remaining cards available.)

Q♣-Q♥-Q♦-7♣-10♥

8) Two Pair
Two sets of two cards which are the same. (Completed by the highest remaining card available.)

6♦-6♥-4♠-4♥-K♣

9) One Pair
Two cards of the same kind. (Completed by the three highest cards available.)

A♦-A♠-Q♥-7♣-4♠

10) High Card
None of the above. Your highest personal card, plus the four highest cards available. remaining cards available.)

A♠-5♠-3♥-10♦-7♦

- ♦ **Flush beats straight.** the hardest thing for beginners to remember is that a *flush* beats a *straight*!

- ♦ **High as a kite.** If you only have a have a high card, the hand is pronounced "X-high," such as in "Ace-high" or "King-high."

Don't Get Outkicked!

If two players have the same pair, then the second hole card matters. Think of it as a tie-breaker. Or a heartbreaker - since it causes you to lose all your money, babe.

It's called **the kicker**.

For example, if you are holding K♦-3♠, and your opponent is holding K♠-Q♣, and you both hit a pair of kings, then they win. You got outkicked!

I'm winning, No You're Winning, No I'm Winning...

Every round can change which hand is winning at that moment.

Take this example:

> **Flop:** Q♦-7♣-5♣
>
> **Theresa:** 7♥-5♥
>
> **Zach:** A♣-10♣

Who's winning? She is! Zach has nothing, while Theresa has two pair.

Now let's see the turn card...

> **Turn:** Q♦-7♣-5♣-K♣
>
> **Theresa:** 7♥-5♥
>
> **Zach:** A♣-10♣

Uh-oh! Now Zach is in the lead. He has a flush.

And the river...

> **River:** Q♦-7♣-5♣-K♣-7♦
>
> **Theresa:** 7♥-5♥
>
> **Zach:** A♣-10♣

Great river card for Theresa - she now has a full house! Her full house beats Zach's flush. You go, girl.

Streetsmart

Back in the day, poker players didn't say "turn" or "river" – they said "fourth street" or "fifth street." Some of the street-talk carries on to this day. A way to describe the hand played above would be to say: "The winner changed on every street."

Most Improved

Some people are like fine wines – they only get better with age. Others... well... peak.

Same with poker hands.

Certain hands are better able to *improve*. This has nothing to do with their self-awareness or ability to incorporate life's lessons. There are simply more cards in the deck which improve their ranking, making upward mobility more probable.

A pair can improve to two-pair. Two pair can improve to a full house. A full house can improve to quads. And so on.

The hand that has the most difficulty improving is a straight. If another player hits a flush or full house, there's nothing the person with the straight can do. For example 6♥-7♣ vs 5♦-5♥ and the flop comes 3♠-4♥-5♣. But the turn is 3♦. The straight now loses to a full house and there is nothing that can be done.) They're *drawing dead* – meaning there is no possible way for their hand to beat the other hand. Their fate is already sealed. Lock 'em up and throw away the key!

Troubleshooting

Sometimes it's hard to determine whose hand is the winner.

In poker and in politics, it's not always right against wrong. The biggest battles are competing truths. Diversity versus unity, equality versus achievement, flush versus straight. Both parties can have a good hand.

But you can always page your poker professor: The Dealer. Turn your hand over at showdown every time just to be sure – the dealer will let you know if yours is best. Card conflicts all have resolutions.

Stop turning your hand over at showdown once you get better at poker and can determine the winner for yourself. Keeping your cards a mystery will give your opponents less information. If they're that curious, tell them "you have to pay to see it." Bet big next time and see how much they really want to see your hand!

Q&A

Q) I have a pair and my opponent has a pair. Who wins?

A) The higher pair 8♣-8♠ beats 7♥-7♦. *The ranking of face cards from highest to lowest is ace, king, queen, jack.*

Q) Can a flush beat a flush?

A) Yes! This is happens all the time especially with "baby flushes." Let's say the board runout is A♦-10♦-7♣-2♦-9♠. You have 6♦-5♦ and your opponent has K♦-Q♦. Their big flush beats your little flush!

Q) Do suits matter?

A) Depends on the dress code.

Q) We both have two pair. Who wins?

A) That's a tricky one! Be very careful here: whoever has the highest pair wins. Let's say the board is A♦-3♠-10♥-K♥-8♠. You have K♣-10♣ and they have A♥-3♣. Who wins? They do. Aces and threes is a better card combo than kings and tens.

Q) What if no one made any matches?

A) The player with the highest card wins. K♦-J♥ will beat 9♠-8♠ if the board is Q♠-7♣-2♥-3♦-10♦.

Counterfeiting

One of the most tragic events in poker is getting **counterfeited** – the board hijcks your hand. There is nothing you can do when this happens, and it is so frustrating you may want to file charges.

Example: you have 9♥-9♣ and Sally has A♣-9♣ with the board being K♠-K♣-J♥-7♦.

Right now you are a huge favorite to win the hand – you have a pair of nines, and Sally has nothing! There is only one card to come.

Which is... K♠-K♣-J♥-7♦-J♦

Oops.

You just got **counterfeited**.

Now Sally's 5-card hand combination is K♠-K♣-J♥-J♦-A♣, which is better than K♠-K♣-J♥-J♦-9♦.

Counterfeiting is not something you have to worry about often, but it does happen. Some hands are more vulnerable to being counter-feited than others – such as aces with a bad kicker (i.e. one of your cards is an ace, and the other card is number less than ten).

A simpler way to think about counterfeiting is knowing there is no such thing as three-pair.

Example: The board runout is 7♥-10♠-10♦-3♦-A♥.

The hand 7♠-3♠ loses to A♣-J♦ because three-pair doesn't exist.

Chop it up!

Chopped pots are like chopped salads – they won't derail your diet, but are a lot less exciting than mac 'n' cheese.

When two players reveal the same hand, they split the winnings equally.

A chopportunity[4] can also happen when the runout equalizes the players' hands – say, giving everyone a straight. Or there can be enough high cards to make kickers irrelevant. Another reason to avoid playing weak aces[5].

None of this is vital information for beginners. Just FYI.

> **Fun Fact**
>
> **If the pot can't be split equally and there's a leftover chip (e.g $51 when the smallest chip is $1), then the extra chip ($1) goes to the player "closest to the dealer button" because they had to undergo the disadvantage of acting first!**

---

4 Chop + opportunity. Credit: poker commentator + comedian Joe Stapleton.

5 "Weak aces" is an ace with a kicker less than ten. A♥-K♣ is a strong ace but A♥-2♣ is a weak ace.

Pokerspeak Dictionary

Pokerspeak is its own unique language consisting of Frankenstein word combos and insider-slang. Why say, "I've got a pair of aces with a king kicker" when you could declare, "I've got top-top!"

Since we're all insatiable braggarts, winning hand jargon is something you will hear on the poker table very, very frequently. Guys love talking about their big... hands.

Here's a list of some of the fun ways to talk poker.

Winner, Winner, Chicken Dinner!

Phrases used for positive hands and experiences. Strokes of good luck.

Top-top – The highest pair and highest kicker. Abbrev. for top pair, top kicker.

Top and bottom – The highest pair and lowest pair.

Trips – Three-of-a-kind, when you have one in your hole cards and the other two are on the board. (Ex. You hold 4♥-3♥ and the flop is 3♦-3♠-A♦)

Set – Three-of-a-kind, when you have two in your hole cards and the other one is on the board. (Ex. You hold 10♠-10♣ and the flop is 10♥-6♣-2♦)

Pet Peeve! Flopping a set and calling it trips.

Boat – Full house.

Broadway – Straight running from 10 through ace. (Ex. If you have Q♠-J♦ and the board is A♥-K♠-4♣-4♠-10♦, congrats, "you made broadway!").

Heater – Hot streak of winning hands.

Run good – consistently making good hands and getting lucky. Everything seems to be working out in your favor.

Nuts – The absolute best possible hand *(see end of this chapter)*.

Luckbox – When you are luckier than that woman who won the lottery four times[1].

Curses!

When you play poker, there will be times when you get un-lucky[2]. As Shakespeare wrote, "the slings and arrows of outra-geous fortune[3]."

Getting outdrawn happens so frequently poker players have their own vocabulary list to articulate *bad beats* - times the "poker gods" bestow great misfortune and doom.

---

1 Joan R. Ginther is a four-time lottery winner. Her first win was for $5.4 million, followed by $2 million, then $3 million, and another $10 million in 2008. The chances of winning the lottery even once is 1 in 200 million – making it more likely to be struck by an asteroid.
2 *Extreme* understatement!
3 Hamlet, Act III.

Drat! Darn! Fiddlesticks!

Phrases used for times of bad luck. My sympathy in advance.

Cooler – When you have an amazing hand that is almost never beat—but is. It's so unlikely your hand is second-best you are bound to lose the maximum. "Sick cooler, man" is often followed by "there's nothing you can do". (ex. 3♣-3♠ vs 4♥-4♣ on 3♦-4♠-J♥ flop.)

Suck-out – Someone outdraws you and wins through dumb luck.

Brick – A deadweight card on the turn or river. (example: K♣-Q♣-J♠-A♣-2♥. The deuce is a total brick.)

Got it in good – Losing your entire chip stack when having done the "right" thing. Usually used to express solace after getting sucked out on ("At least I got it in good!")

Backdoor – An improbable two consecutive cards on the turn and river completing a hand. (Ex. 2♥-6♣-K♠ flop followed by turn card 3♥ and river can 5♥ will cause Rob's K♦-K♣ to lose to Samantha's backdoor flush with 7♥-4♥)

Runner-runner – Same as backdoor.

Run bad – Repeatedly getting unlucky.

Rivered – When the river changes your hand from winner to loser.

Stacked – Losing your entire stack to another person. The spy who stacked me!

Felted – Losing all your chips. (Ex. "I just got felted.") Your money is one with the table felt, never to return[4].

Let's Go Nuts!

It is no secret that poker is a male-dominated game. And if there was ever any doubt, the best possible hand in poker at any given time is called *the nuts*.

---

4 Dramatic characterization.

Nut-terminology is a science in its own right.

"Nut straight," "nut flush," "nut no pair[5]," "second nuts," "third nuts," "fourth nuts," "nut draw," "nuts with the nut redraw," and "nutted" are all examples of totally common and socially acceptable table talk.

"The nut straight" means the best possible straight. "Second nuts" means the second-best possible hand. Nothing can beat the nuts. Except icy cold swimming pools.

Whenever you hear "nut" or "nuts," substitute "best possible."

A cooler commonly involves the second nuts losing to the nuts.

Nutology

No one knows exactly how the term "nuts" was invented, but there are two major theories.

Back in the wild, wild west, poker-playing cowboys on the American frontier weren't the biggest fans of rules. They made the game a little... more flexible. You weren't limited to only wagering the chips you had on the table; you could bet your left arm if you wanted to. And you could even add-on more money or valuables right in the middle of a hand.

Cowboys would put up their horse and wagon - requiring them to *remove the nuts from their wagon wheels*. That way they can't bolt if they lose their bet. Old-fashioned insurance.

The thinking was that no one would commit their wagon-wheel nuts without with the best possible poker hand.

Alternatively, you can subscribe to the *Oxford English Dictionary* definition, which says being "nuts to" a person is "a source of pleasure or delight to one."

---

5 Best possible hand without having a pair.

Meet the Cards

There is a popular trend online where YouTube gurus order a "mystery box" off Ebay and unpack it on-camera – discovering whatever they just purchased for anywhere from $100 to $10,000.

A mystery box is a box that could be filled with... well... anything.

Which means it's usually junk.

The same goes with cards.

The first peek at your cards provides a mini rush, until you realize most of your hands are destined for **the muck** – poker's trash pile. The muck is a sloppy card dump next to the dealer for all the rejects. It's the Island of Lost Toys, except without any cool Disney polishing. No amount of magic will make mucked cards return to real life: Once they're in the muck, they're gone forever[1]. And good riddance! You don't want mucked cards anyways.

PRO TIP

Whenever someone asks me how to get better at poker, I always say, "FOLD!"

The best way to get better at poker is to fold more.

Truth is, most poker hands are awful. Statistical miscreants. Mathematical losers. That one D-list celebrity who can just never seem to get it together. Depending on the stakes you are playing, you may as well be spending hundreds of dollars only to unveil random clutter. Or, as the eBay-YouTubers say, "unbox."

Slim Pickings
You're only supposed to play 15-20% of hands.

---

1 The only time cards can be removed from the muck is when they have been turned face-up and caught on-camera in a tournament situation. Otherwise, no backsies.

The Three Types

There are three types of hands you should play - and fold everything else. You need to be picky. No, not like in your dating life. I mean actually picky.

Face cards

A picture is worth a thousand words – and maybe a thousand dollars. Any two cards with an ace or face – king, queen, jack – are better than the rest. Skin for the win.

Pairs

Ahh – the easiest to play! Simple and profitable, two-of-a-kind grant peace of mind.

Suited connectors

Two cards of the same suit and numerically connected. These are a bit trickier to play and can easily be folded. But love is love, and sometimes you need to mess around with a guy who's a bit of a "project."

Just Face it

Picture cards – known as face cards – are king, queen, jack. And also ace. They are the most valuable cards in poker, because we should always keep our eyes on a person's... face.

It's Polly Pocket!

When two of your hole cards match, it's called a *pocket pair*. This is great because you already have what's called a "made hand" – you don't need to connect with the flop! A pair is a pair and no can take that away from you. Not even the government.

Sorry, I'm not good with numbers...

Number cards are the hardest to play because they are much less likely to be the best hand at showdown – *meaning you will have to bluff and make moves*. They require more skill.

Here's why.

a) You will need to be confident playing draws.

Let's say you have 8♠-9♠ and the flop is A♠-K♠-4♥. Sure, another spade will improve you to a flush and most likely give you the winning hand – but what do you if another spade doesn't hit? You're going to need to have a back-up plan.

b) You will often have the second-best hand.

Let's say you have 8♠-9♠ again, and the flop is A♥-3♥-9♣. Do you have the best hand? Hard to say. You might with a pair of nines, but anyone with an ace beats you. It's going to be hard to know what to do – even if you're a pro!

Number cards are there for a reason[2]. If you only played face cards and pairs, you would be too predictable. They can also make fantastic winning hands on occasion – with the benefit of disguise.

Master of Disguise

Suited cards are like men in suits – they look a lot more exciting than they really are. Number cards can make the best hand – in a style that's very tricky! Imagine having 5♦-2♦ on a A♣-3♦-4♠ flop, and your opponent has A♠-A♥. Look closely. They have three aces, but you have a straight! Concealed and deadly.

---

2 Unless you are playing short-deck/six-plus hold'em – a trendy new game where all the cards lower than a six are removed. It's all the rage in Asia!

What If It's Suited?

Any time you're dealt two cards of the same suit (spades, clubs, hearts, or diamonds), your hand is automatically "suited[3]." If only clothes shopping was so easy!

Many players look down at J♥-3♠ and can tell it's a gross and should be folded. But when they see J♥-3♥, their palms get sweaty, their faces flush, and they're just as jittery as that time the cute guy from the dog park texted back that very same day.

Sorry to break it to you, but most suited cards – and most random guys! – don't work out.

Holding two suited cards raises the value of your hand by only 3%. You wouldn't pay extra for 3% fewer ads or 3% faster internet or makeup that's 3% organic. Suited cards are like a marketing ploy – they're not really premium.

That's not the worst of it though. They will also put you in very tricky spots.

---

3 Likewise, if your two cards are differing in suits, then your hand is automatically "off-suit." Someone might say "Ace-king off-suit" to describe a hand like A♥-K♣." They may even just say, "Ace-king off." Another reason why so many men lack finesse in talking about clothing.

Let's say you have J♥-3♥ and the flop is A♥-K♥-2♣. Again, it's going to be an extra difficult challenge to win this hand if another heart doesn't hit – which usually isn't going to happen.

This means most of the time you are going to be hoping for something that's never going to happen. Sorry, babe.

Random suited cards create awkward situations where you have a very low pair, or top pair with a bad kicker. *You'll constantly find yourself guessing* if your hand is winning in very close spots. Save your brainpower.

PRO TIP

Flush draws on the flop will only complete by the river around 35% of the time.

> **My biggest mistake when I first started playing poker was calling big pre-flop reraises with suited aces.**

Shopping at the GAP

Lastly, you will be dealt "gappers." These are cards which are connected enough to make a straight, but don't immediately follow each other. Like 10♣-8♠, 9♥-7♥, or 6♦-4♣. Those are called one-gappers. Two-gappers are hands like 8♠-5♠. Don't ask about three-gappers – we don't go there!

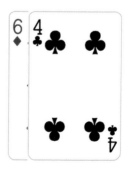

Girl's Guide Starter Pack

Last chapter we learned that playable cards fall into three catego-ries: **face cards**, **pocket pairs**, and **suited connectors**. Everything else is junk! Like junk mail, it's better left ignored.

How to Stay Out of Trouble

Life consists of many important decisions – where to live, what career to pursue, and is he Mr. Right or are we settling? Each with varying degrees of importance and impact (I sound like a mom!)

In poker, the most crucial decisions you make will be pre-flop.

Choosing which cards to play sets the tone for the future.

Maniac gamblers like to play lots of cards and see lots of flops, throwing caution – and profit! – to the wind. They have what is called a **wide range** of hands. Less experienced players should limit their card selection to the tried and true, the easier to play and con-sistently profitable, the Old Faithfuls of Texas Hold 'Em. Beginners should stick to a **tight range**. Like, really tight. Smaller than Barbie's waist tight.

Best Poker Hands

Below are the top five best starting hands in poker.

You can play them at any time at any seat; they're so good, posi-tion doesn't matter. They have the highest probabilities of being the best hand at showdown, and don't require fancy maneuvers or advanced bluffs. Much of the time they just, like, win.

Play these hands anytime, anywhere, any place.

The following *almost* made the cut.

They're the next tier down.

The Official Girl's Guide Starter Pack

A Girl's Guide to Poker explains position before which cards to play – because you should decide which cards to play based on your seat. There is a Yiddish saying "*a velt in kleine velts*" which means "a world in little worlds." Which cards to play is cocooned in the theory of position; a world within another world.

The "top 5" list includes cards you can play from anywhere – but what about the rest of the deck? Here's a guide for the hands that are more borderline. *(Note: "o" stands for offsuit, and "s" for suited. Each position is cumulative and includes the cards from earlier.)*

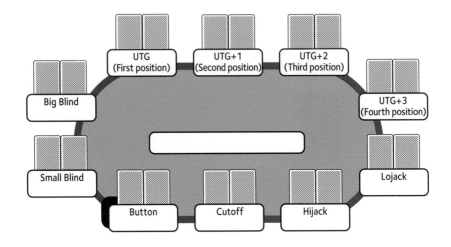

- ♦ **Under-the-Gun (UTG):** AA, KK, AKs, AKo, AQs, AQo, QQ, KQs, JJ, AJs, AJo, ATs, TT, 99, 88, 77.

- ♦ **UTG+1:** add KQo, KJs, QJs.

- ♦ **UTG+2:** add KJo, KTs, 66.

- ♦ **Middle Position 1:** add ATo, A9s, JTs, 55.

- ♦ **MP 2:** add QJo, QTs, J9s,10-9s.

- ♦ **Hijack:** add A5s, KTo,10-8s, 98s,44, 33, 22.

- ♦ **Cutoff:** add A9o, K9s, 97s, 87s, 86s,76s, 75s, 56s, 54s, 53s.

- ♦ **Button:** add all remaining aces.

This is a general guideline. You do not need to follow it exactly.

Most pre-flop raise charts in books and on the internet follow these same recommendations and differ only slightly[1].

---

1 Need help? Try using the pre-flop flashcard trainer on my site amandasaces.com.

A GIRL'S GUIDE TO POKER

What if I don't want to follow these rules?

Poker is for you – play the game you want to play. This is just a foundation. These starting hand ranges apply universally to any table; sometimes 100% optimal strategy will require playing a bit tighter or looser. Use these as intended: a starter pack.

Types of Players

There is no police force in poker – you can play whichever hands you want. No "Officer Spades" is looking over your shoulder.

Poker players each develop their own original style, landing somewhere on the spectrum between tight and loose. Tight players favor a conservative approach – playing the book (or list!). Loose players are "loosened up," and play more cards in more positions. Both styles come with their own pros and cons.

By sticking to only the most reliable cards, tight players avoid tough situations. They don't constantly have to evaluate if their hand is best or decide whether to gamble (translation: they avoid tricky math problems). The upside of playing it safe is that it will be harder to lose; it's playing poker as a computer. Downside is that it's predictable.

PRO TIP

Good tight players *only* play around 15% of their hands. Good loose players play around 30% – double!
Even very loose players still fold the majority of their cards.

Loose players are dangerous. They are hard to read, and, because they play so many hands,seem to have a remarkable knack for getting lucky. Even if they are successful, expect wild swings: profits and losses.

Let's Play!

The past few chapters provided a piecemeal perspective on poker – now it's time for the grand mix-and-match! Taking all the game-play know-how and winning hand rankings to the felt. As the fairy godmother sings in Cinderella, *"Put them together and what have you got? Bibbidi-bobbidi-boo!"*

Alyssa Smart is a savvy poker player who knows what she's doing. Be like Alyssa.

Lila Lackadaisical is a beginner who is all sorts of dazed and con-fused. Makes rookie mistakes. Poor girl.

Kyle Kewl is an average player whose surfer boy hair is much more interesting than his poker game. He plays so-so and will neither win or lose much. But his modeling career looks promising.

The purpose of this section is so you can get a sense of how a poker hand unfolds[1] in real time. Don't get caught up in the numbers or stack sizes – the lesson here is the *sequence of events*.

(For all hands, figure they are among other players seated at a nine-handed poker table. The blinds are $2/$5 and everyone has around $500.)

Example 1

Alyssa Smart raises under-the-gun (UTG) to $20 with A♦-K♥.

Kyle Kewl calls from the button with J♠-10♠.

Lila Lackadaisical calls from the small blind (SB) with 9♥-5♥.

Pot: $65 Flop: A♥-3♣-5♠

Lila checks.

Alyssa bets $30 with her ace.

Kyle folds.

Lila calls with her five.

Pot: $125 Turn: A♥-3♣-5♠-Q♥

Lila checks.

Alyssa bets $75.

Lila calls – she is extra excited now about that second heart! (♥!)

Pot: $275 River: A♥-3♣-5♠-Q♥-8♠

Lila checks.

Alyssa thinks for a moment. She's right on the fence between betting and checking. A check would be playing it safe in case Lila has a better hand. But Alyssa is pretty sure she's winning and decides to go for max value: she bets $100.

Lila feels sick. She's pretty sure her measly pair of fives are losing,

1 Get it?

but has so much invested! Now there is $375 in the pot and it's $100 to see Alyssa's cards. Lila shrugs and makes the call. She loses.

> ### No More "Ladies, first!"
>
> Poker games have a natural flow, and this includes almost always checking to the pre-flop raiser on the flop. When you raise pre-flop, you're telling the other players the story that you have a good hand. They will usually check to you on the flop expecting you to continue your story by betting.

Example 2

Kyle Kewl raises from middle position 1 to $20 with K♦-J♣.

Lila Lackadaisical calls from middle position 2 with A♣-2♦.

Alyssa Smart calls from the button with 8♣-8♠.

Pot: $65 Flop: A♥-K♣-8♦

Kyle bets $30 with his king.

Lila calls with her ace.

Alyssa raises to $100 with her set of eights.

Kyle folds.

Lila calls.

Pot: $325 Turn: A♥-K♣-8♦-7♠

Lila checks.

Alyssa bets $200.

Lila calls.

Pot: $725 River: A♥-K♣-8♦-7♠-K♠

Alyssa says "all-in" (bets $280).

PRO TIP
Think about these hands. What are some things that Lila could've done better? What traits make Kyle a so-so player?

Pot: $1,005.

In order for Lila to see Alyssa's hand, she would have to pay all her chips. There is already around $1,000 in the pot and Lila only has $280 left. She sighs and calls – Alyssa wins with her full house.

Example 3

Lila Lackadaisical limps (aka calls) UTG+1 for $5 with 6♥-5♦.

Kyle Kewl limps from the cutoff (CO) for $5 with K♦-10♠.

Alyssa Smart folds from the SB with A♥-8♣.

Pot: $28 Flop: 2♦-6♣-6♠

Lila bets $25.

Kyle folds.

Lila was practically bursting out of her chair! Even surfer bro Kyle knew to fold – he figured since she only put in $5 pre-flop, it's more likely she has a low number card like a six. Good fold, Kyle.

Size Matters

Betting poker chips is like shopping at Victoria's Secret – one size does not fit all. Sizing correctly is an art form, giving the hand its shape. I'll take a lace push-up.

Proper bet and raise sizing starts pre-flop – especially when there are limpers!

A standard pre-flop raise size is 3x the big blind but you will need to modify depending on whether several players limp or are call-happy. If only poker was easy!

Live casino games will usually have players raising a bit bigger, and online tables favor 2.2-2.5x (button-clicking is easier than chip-counting). Tournament bets and raises may also be sized a bit smaller, in the 2.2–2.5x range.

Avoid the minraise! One of the biggest faux paus in poker is minraising – exactly doubling a raise ($2 to $4). It's not the most profit-

able way to play, and people will make fun of you for it, laughing secretly or overtly. Don't have people snickering under their breath or in your face. Don't minraise.

Always raise bigger if there are limpers!

Generally, you can raise one big blind for every limper in the pot – if one person limped ahead of you at a $1/2 game, raise to $8 instead of $6. Adjustments may need to be made on the fly, but always raise larger if many people limped in front of you. Whether you raise to $7 or $10 is a game-time decision. When in doubt, bigger is better.

PRO TIP
Poker is much easier to play with fewer people in the hand. The cheaper it is to see a flop, the more people will come along for the ride – making it much less likely for you to win. **Size up!**

Reraise **sizing is its own science! Think anywhere from 3x-5x.**

The Legend Continues

When you raise pre-flop, you are telling the story you have a good hand. Post-flop, people expect you to continue with that story – as you often should. And you want the sequel to be even better than the original.

If you were the pre-flop raiser, betting after the flop is called a continuation bet, or **c-bet**.

Do this when facing only a few opponents (ideally just one, or two at most), because it's more likely you have the best hand or can get away with a bluff. It's nearly impossible to bluff five players – and unnecessary. No one needs to bluff five players or date five boyfriends. Too much work!

Continue the Story

Adjust your c-bet size to flop texture (translation: change how much you bet based on the board).

Dry Flop: Bet Small, 1/3-pot
K♣-8♠-3♥ is a very "dry" flop since there aren't any flush draws or straight draws. Players will either have a pairor they won't; there isn't a point in betting big.

Continue the story

Normal Board: Bet 1/2-pot
A♦-3♦-J♠ is a pretty typical flop. There's a flush draw, some likely pairs, and a few one-card ("gutshot") straight draws (e.g. a hand like K♣-Q♠ needs a ten for a straight, or 4♣-5♣ needs a deuce). The cards are somewhat coordinated.

Wet Board: 80%-pot to Full Pot Plus
8♠-7♠-6♠ is the kind of board that gives poker players nightmares. It is extremely coordinated and will connect dangerously with many hands. There are plenty of likely pairs, two pairs, sets, pair plus

straight draws, straight draws, pair plus flush draws, and flush draw combos. If you have a strong hand, bet big.

Bet larger on "wet" coordinated boards to charge draws.

Standard c-bet size is 1/2-pot.

What a Girl Wants

The most important thing to keep in mind when betting is knowing what you want. Do you want people to call? Choose a size you think they will pay. Do you want them to fold? Don't bet too small then – make it extra large so they toss away all their "maybe baby" hands. Sizing may seem random when you're first starting – and that's okay. Focus on your intention rather than exact numbers. Try and decide what you want to have happen (get calls or get folds), because that thought process will come in handy for the future. Think ahead!

All the Odds

Eighty-four percent of statistics are fake. These ones aren't.

Here is your ultimate resource for every probability in No-Limit Hold'em. *This chapter should be marked.* Fold the corner, kiss the title. Study it harder than Elle Woods[1] in *Legally Blonde* did to get into Harvard. Skip to the quick list on *page 99*.

Quiz yourself on poker odds on my website amandasaces.com.

The most important statistic to know is that you will miss the flop 2/3 of the time.

PRO TIP

There are plenty of free poker apps where you can plug in your cards and see who's most likely to win.

Definite poker must-have.

I don't like percentages!

An alternate way to look at your hand's chances of winning is calculating "outs." Think of how many cards are available in the deck to give you the best hand. If you need to hit an open-ended straight draw for example, then you have eight outs.

For example you hold 7♣-6♣ and the flop is 9♦-8♥-3♠. Any five or ten will make you a straight. There are four fives in the deck and four tens, meaning you have eight cards to hit for the winner.

Note: All statistics are calculated for draws completing by the river unless otherwise stated.

---

1 My personal hero and role model.

Flip City!

Most people don't get rich flipping homes, and you'll never get rich "coin flipping" in poker. A pocket pair versus two overcards is called a **flip**, because the odds are about 50/50. Get all your money in pre-flop with A♦-K♣ against 2♦-2♥, and the likelihood of either hand winning is near even – with pocket deuces a slight favorite. The pair is always a sliver ahead, but for the most part the winner is anyone's guess. Tournament poker may make you topsy turvy because it's full of flips![2]

Other examples of flips:

2 I'm still waiting for the poker book that teaches me how to win my flips!

Don't Hunt Diamonds

Most of the time when you flop a flush draw and are praying for that next diamond, spade, heart, or spade, it's mostly not going to happen.

Flush draws only complete 35% of the time.

If you have J♦-10♦ and the flop is A♦-3♠-4♦, another diamond card is coming (either on the turn or river) only around a third of the time.

You will only flop a flush one time in 118.

The Straight and Narrow

Making an **open-ended straight** is a smidge harder than hitting a flush – the odds are 32%. An "open-ender" draw looks something like holding 7♠-6♥ and the flop is 9♦-8♥-2♣.

The reason why a straight is a rarer than a flush is that there are always 8 cards you can hit for your open-ender (5♣, 5♦, 5♠, 5♥ or 10♣, 10♦, 10♠, 10♥), but nine flush cards.

The sneakiest kind of straight to hit is a **gutshot** – you've got a straight draw on just one side. That would look like having 7♠-6♥ on a 10♠-8♥-2♣ flop – only a nine will make your straight. The

likelihood of hitting a gutshot is close to 15% (technically 16.5%). Some people call this a gutter, because those that outdraw you in such a way may as well be from the underworld.

Open-ended straight draw: 32%

Gutshot: 16%

Eyes Up Here!

When thinking about how many "outs" you have – how many cards you can hit to make the winning hand – it's worthwhile to consider **overcards**. Maybe you've got a little help up there.

If you have A♦-J♦ and the flop is K♦-5♦-2♠, you still have a 35% of hitting another diamond. Let's say your opponent has K♠-Q♠ – how does that affect your chances of winning?

Since an ace will give you the best hand even the another diamond doesn't come, your equity jumps – in this case to around 46%. Whenever one of your overcards is "live," your equity will always increase to more than 40%.

Pokerspeak: "I went-all in on a flush draw, but was sure my ace was live."

Be wary your overcards will not always be enough. In the A♦-J♦ example, turning or rivering an ace would not win if the other player's hand was A♣-K♠. Your heart may skip a beat when you see that ace, but it's tainted love!

Overcards can give you a mathematical edge – even if you haven't hit anything yet!

For example you hold K♥-Q♣ and the opponent has 7♠-7♣ on a flop of J♦-10♠-3♣.

Any ace or nine will make you a straight and any king or queen will make you a pair. The odds now are 53% vs 47% *in your favor*. Life works in mysterious ways.

Calculating overcard outs can be tricky because you need to know the other person's hand. X-ray vision required.

Combo Draws

Fries and a coke supersize any Happy Meal[3]. A combo draw super-sizes any poker hand. Fatten my wallet, please!

Up above we discussed how an ace being live juices any draw significantly – and that's just the beginning. A live overcard adds three additional outs[4]. Gutshot straight draws add four. The best kind of combo draw – a flush and straight draw – is a serious force to be reckoned with. Worth your all-in.

Whenever you flop a monster combo draw, go with it.

Holding 9♠-8♠ and seeing 10♠-J♠-4♥ is akin to flopping the world. Plug this into your handy poker calculator app, and you'll find that you're a (slight) mathematical favorite even against A♦-A♥!

Three cheers for a combo draw! A straight + flush draw completes 54% – making it a mathematical favorite against nearly anything.

A pair + flush draw is also strong. Let's say the flop is J♣-5♠-4♠. How does J♠-10♠ fare against K♦-K♥?

It's a virtual coin flip – 49.80% vs 50.20%.

Play these combinations aggressively because it balances your raises when you have hands like sets.

The truth is, most solo straight or flush draws won't hit – that's why it's important to have extra outs. Combo draws and additional pair opportunities give life-lines – providing insurance to rescue you.

---

3 McDonald's please sponsor.
4 There are four of every card in the deck. Already holding one in your hand means there are three left for you to hit.

The Multi-Million Dollar Decision

The year is 2006, when the WSOP was at peak popularity. Poker's biggest championship – The Main Event – was down to the last three standing out of 8,773 entrants. First prize was $12,000,000. The flop was 10♣-6♠-5♠.

Michael Binger has A♥-10♥ (29% equity).

Jamie Gold has 4♠-3♣ (17% equity).

Paul Wasicka has 8♠-7♠ (54% equity).

Binger commits virtually all his chips with his top pair. Gold goes all-in with his straight draw. Now Wasicka has a decision.

Should he risk all his chips on a big combo draw?

(Wasicka can hit either a straight or flush).

Wasicka is mathematically most likely to win. But 54% is just slightly better than a coin flip. And the pay jumps are huge. First place wins $12,000,000. Second wins $6,102,499. Third wins $4,123,310. Not to mention sponsorship opportunities accompanying the title – estimates value this at another 7 to 10 million dollars[5].

Bare minimum, this is a 2-million-dollar decision (the pay jump between second place and third), for a hand you win a little more than 50/50. That's enough to make anyone queasy. What would you do?

An extremely distressed Wasicka eventually made the fold. And yes, he would've won the hand. Wasicka finished the tournament in second place. It's possible Wasicka wondered if one of his opponents had a better flush draw – say, K♠-Q♠ – in which case his equity shrivels from 54% to 31%.

---

5 Estimate by The Poker Guys who have an excellent YouTube channel and podcast.

One Pair, Two Pair

We can't always head the pack; sometimes it's best to be awarded "Most Improved." That's what my high school sports medals say anyway.

Whenever you flop a pair, it will improve to two-pair or trips around 25% of the time.

That means if the flop is J♥-7♦-5♣, your 8♠-7♠ will beat another player's K♠-J♦ roughly one in every four times.

Three-of-a-kind

Good things come in threes, but threes rarely come! The math says you'll flop a set one in every 8.5 times. For example Q♦-J♥-2♠ flop when you have 2♣-2♠. This translates to roughly 12%.

Pair the Board!

Miracle of miracles you flopped a set – but someone else flopped a straight! Uh-oh. You're now going to need to improve to a full house to win. The board will pair – giving you a boat[6] – 35% of the time. Not all hope is lost!

For example if the flop is 6♠-7♥-8♣. Mindy's set of 7♣-7♠ will beat Tyler's 10♠-9♠ straight approximately one in every three times (35%).

Counterfeited

When someone flops low two pairs, they can get counterfeited by another player's cards.

Aaron's 7♣-6♣ beats Matt's Q♣-Q♠ on a 6♠-7♥-3♦ flop, because Aaron's two pair is better than Matt's one pair. But if the runout is

---

6 Slang for full house.

6♠-7♥-3♦-J♦-3♣, the tables have turned. Matt now has a higher two pair (queens and threes). Counterfeiting happens 25% of the time .

My Cards Versus Your Cards

A hand such as A♦-K♠ vs 10♠-9♠ is a classic 60/40 spot in ace-king's favor.

Pair versus one overcard is 70/30 as in 8♦-8♥ vs K♥-6♣.

Outkicked varies between 65/45 and 70/30 such as Q♣-J♠ versus J♦-10♥.

Don't be Mad at Me!

My first time playing poker at a casino with my dad. We'd been playing for a few hours and he started racking up his chips getting ready to leave. I looked down at my last hand: K♣-K♠.

An extremely wild and reckless player raised pre-flop, and I reraised.

He responded: "All-in."

I looked up at my dad sheepishly and said, "Please don't be mad at me!" and made the call.

The board came A♦-3♠-8♥-7♣-J♥.

The wild guy turned over A♥-K♦ and scoops the pot. Pre-flop I was a 70% favorite.

I looked back up at my dad again saying, "I'm sorry Dad, I had to call."

He responded, "I'd be more upset if you didn't."

Thoughts on Floating

Sometimes players "float the flop" if one of their overcards hasn't hit, like calling a bet with A♦-Q♠ when the flop is 3♦-10♠-5♣ in case an ace or queen comes on the turn. Generally, it's not a good idea to get too sticky. Floating doesn't usually work. How often will A♦-Q♠ win against J♣-10♣ on that flop? Around 25% – and that's assuming hanging around to see both turn and river. Best to just let it go.

Weird Two Pairs

People like to get cute and play wacky cards because if they hit two pair, nobody will see it coming. That's true – I'm never going to expect someone to be holding a hand like J♦-3♣. But I'll take my chances: the odds of flopping two pair are 2%.

Will I Ever Hit?

Poker can be as frustrating as dating. Try as you might, you can't find a true connection. Will your cards ever find a flop that's a match?

Generally, no. Most of the time you won't flop a pair – let alone a straight or flush.

Remember that you will miss the flop 2/3 of the time.

But that doesn't mean you should force it. Don't play junky cards out of frustration (that's called gambling), and don't convince yourself to kiss too many frogs. Poker takes patience. And skill! Once you learn how to outplay people, they'll never know if you smashed the flop or not.

Girl's Guide Odds Master List

- Flopping a pair… 29%
- Flopping two pair… 2%
- Flopping a set… 12%
- Flopping a flush… 0.84%
- Flopping a straight with two connected hole cards… 1.3%
- Making a flush by the river… 35%
- Making an open-ended straight by the river… 32%
- Making a gutshot straight by the river… 16%
- Making a full house by the river after flopping a set… 33%
- Pocket pair vs two overcards… 51%
- Lower pocket pair against higher pocket pair… 18%
- Pair vs one overcard… 70%
- Kicker pairing… 25%
- Pairing either overcard after the flop… 25%

The Truth about Small Stakes Poker

Word to the wise before moving onto the next chapters: they're covering a different genre of poker. More advanced poker. More sophisticated poker. *Real poker.* A game weaving captivating storylines, and all about pressure. Not to mention an extreme reverence for anything sly.

There is one big difference between high and low stakes poker, which completely changes the way the game is played: *showdown.*

The more expensive it is to play, the less people will pay to see your cards. For $30, they'll call your bet with many things. For $300, far fewer things.

Then there's the blinds. Lower stakes games are shorter stacked; you have less relative (and actual!) chips to mess around with and pull fancy maneuvers. It's hard to "triple-barrel"[1] bluff when someone has already committed most of their stack. When they feel *pot-commited* – they've invested too much now to fold –

---

1 Poker term for bluffing three times; on flop, turn, and river.

the hands they call down with will be much weaker. Like your friend who's been with the same guy since high school, she'll be reluctant to leave. Even if the play is not usually correct.

An Example of Small Stakes Play

Better Becca with a stack of $300 has K♥-Q♠.

Ginger Gee with a stack of $120 has 10♦-8♣.

Ginger is not a very good player. She's playing a $3/$5 game, and open limps 10♦-8♣ from the hijack. Becca is better and raises to $20. The flop is A♠-10♠-5♣ and the pot is $48.

Ginger checks, and Becca bets $20. This is a board that strongly favors Becca's story – she can very easily have an ace since she raised pre-flop. All broadway combinations – kings, queens, jacks, and tens – have a gutshot straight draw. A spade on the turn also gives her a queen-high flush draw. That makes this hand an excellent candidate

to *barrel*[2]. Especially because Ginger's story is quite weak – she either has a bad ace, or a middling strength hand like a 10 (which she does). Any better hand she likely would've raised.

Becca bets $20. Ginger calls.

The turn brings A♠-10♠-5♣-7♥ and the pot is $88.

Ginger checks. Now Becca is in a lousy situation. Most poker pros would keep betting here, and any proper poker book would tell you that Becca should keep betting as a general rule. But Ginger only has $60 left – less than what is already in the pot. Ginger may think her ten is no good if Becca bets again, but she already feels married to the pot ("pot committed!") and is never folding. The hand will inevitably reach showdown, and Becca will most likely lose.

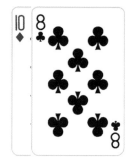

Becca did not do anything wrong pre-flop. She got the other player to commit her money as a statistical loser – the math is more than 60/40 in her favor. Repeat the hand 1,000x and Becca will surely come out a winner.

But this is not real poker. It's just playing the numbers. It's a math game.

Post-flop neither player can really outplay the other. They can't apply pressure on different run-outs, they can't effectively semi-bluff. *Whoever hits wins.*

In this scenario, both players were painfully short-stacked – which is not uncommon at these stakes. Many $3/$5 games have a

2 Bet all three streets.

$100-$300 buy-in. That means whenever someone flops an even half-decent pair or draw, they're usually closing their eyes and going with it – which is as bad as mystery drinks at a frat party. Don't sip the jungle juice. Don't play the $3/$5.

Beating low stakes poker is a math game.

Name Your Price

Aspiring poker players always ask me about body language, facial tells, and, most of all, bluffing. They think the key is having a good poker face. The truth is, all that is overrated. Many times you can turn your cards face-up and it wouldn't really matter.

Let's say you have 9♥-8♥ and I have A♣-K♠. The flop is 9♠-A♦-7♥.

I could show you my hand, and you wouldn't fold right away to my bet. You'd ask, "how much?"

♥♥ Quiz Level Two: Hearts ♥♥

Keep track of your answers. Correct answers are worth 10 points!

1) Circle the (3) game selection deal-breakers.

2) Everyone takes turns in poker, rotating...

a) To the Right.

b) *"To the left, to the left, everything you own in a box to the left!"* Beyoncé lyrics finally taught me something.

3) How many hole cards are you given in No-Limit Hold'em?

a) Two, duh.

b) Three.

c) Five.

d) What's a hole card again?

4) Is it an advantage to be first to act or last to act?

a) First!

b) Last. Nice girls finish last.

5) Does position matter?

a) Yes, you can play more hands in late position.

b) No, I'm happy where I'm at.

6) What is "Under the Gun"?

a) How it feels driving through rush hour.

b) The first person to act pre-flop, left of the big blind.

c) Sounds like a Jake Gyllenhaal movie.

7) Which of the following is not a reason to raise?

a) Generate more money in the pot.

b) Smoke out weak hands.

c) Establish the betting lead.

d) Impress the boys with your moxie.

8) True or false: you will miss the flop most of the time.

a) True. Two-thirds of the time to be exact.

b) False. I won't miss the flop, and I won't miss my ex-boyfriend.

9) When in doubt, how large should your continuation bet be?

a) Half pot.

b) Full pot.

c) Pot? Who's got weed?

d) I'm too chicken to c-bet.

10) What is "checking the nuts"?

a) Haha, ew.

b) Not betting when you have the best possible hand.

c) Once again, ew.

11) True or False: Real women re-raise.

a) True, I'm badass.

b) False, I'm not badass.

Answers on page 203.

All the Ra(n)ge

The poker universe is bursting with different theories and ideas for how to play optimally. Logic scions believe the game can ultimately be solved; it's a puzzle that can be mastered by a computer. The idea of "perfect poker." The poker community calls this *game theory optimal* (or "GTO" if you want to sound cool/nerdy). Then there are the traditionalists who believe poker is a game of adapting to individual styles – playing in a way that *exploits* rather than removes human nature.

Rock, Paper, Scissors!

The classic way to think about GTO versus exploitative strategy is the game rock, paper, scissors.

Game theory optimal strategy says you should pick each option equally, making you perfectly balanced and impossible to predict. But if your opponent always picks scissors, exploitative theory says you should adapt to their weakness by always picking rock – even if it makes you imbalanced and less tricky.

As the game evolves and conventional poker knowledge improves – your dad didn't have a poker odds calculator app on his smartphone – body language reading and "going with your gut" is becoming a thing of the past. The last thing on many current pro poker players' minds is getting better at decoding facial tells. Keeping up with the times means mastering the terms **balance**, **blockers** and **range**. Modern poker commentators won't say, "What a convincing bluff!" They'll say, "She has an extreme range advantage."

I'm going to make a wild assumption and guess you're not a high stakes poker pro whose decisions are analyzed on-camera. You probably don't have to worry about multimillionaire cardsharks preying on your decisions and realizing you're most likely to choose scissors in rock, paper, scissors. It's okay if you're not perfectly balanced.

But you should grasp one new age concept: **Range**.

I wouldn't feel right sending you to a poker table otherwise – I'd be a bad poker mama!

PRO TIP
Poker storytelling is much clearer when you think in terms of ranges.

Ranging Ranges

A range is the variety of cards a person is likely to play pre-flop.

What's your **spectrum?**

Beginners, Billionaires and Drunks
Beginners, billionaires, and drunks usually have the widest ranges. They aren't playing poker to be profitable; they're playing for fun, which means playing as many hands as possible. Ever heard the expression "anything with a pulse" or "anything that walks"? This is the pre-flop equivalent. These types of players have never met a hand they didn't like. When you're trying to figure out their cards, be on the lookout for wacky two pairs and silly straights. Everything is fair game. *Likely range: Any two cards in the deck.*

Older Players

Poker used to be far less aggressive back in the day (reraises weren't really a thing), which is why older poker players tend to have a very narrow range. Mostly picture cards and aces. When deducing what their cards are, it's unlikely for them to have a hand like 6♠-4♠. What's their type? Anything with a face – applying to both cards that is. Headshots only! *Likely range: aces and faces.*

Poker Students

Next-gen students of the game cling to pre-flop charts like it's their religion. They play textbook poker – what is most mathematically profitable – based on position. The other players types tend to play the same cards in any seat. These don't. Different cards at different times. Also no face cards with bad kickers or offsuit number cards. *A Girl's Guide* is a member of this church. *Likely range: Check the chart.*

> **Back in the day, there was a saying "no set, no bet."**
> **Poker was so conservative that players didn't even bet**
> **unless they had three-of-a-kind. Minimum!**

Why All the Fuss?

People at a poker table are always, always, always representing a hand. They're telling you they have a good hand. Or a bad hand. Or a so-so hand. Without a sense of range, you won't know if a hand is good or bad.

Poker is not my cards against your cards, but my range against your range.

Home on the Range

A pre-flop raiser's range always skews towards pocket pairs and face cards. Everyone plays those from every position. Especially big pocket pairs like A♦-A♥ or K♣-K♠. People who just call pre-flop have many hands with a queen or jack or suited connectors. They're not supposed to have a high pocket pair or a strong ace because it's smarter to reraise those hands pre-flop.

Take a look at these flops. Which one is likely to favor the pre-flop raiser's range? The caller's?

a) A♥-K♣-6♦

b) 5♣-6♣-9♦

The answer is (a).

If you guessed that (a) gives the edge to the pre-flop raiser and (b) to the pre-flop caller, you are correct! Clever girl.

Let's Pretend

You raise 9♥-8♥ in middle position.

Flop is A♥-K♣-6♦.

If you continuation-bet this flop as a bluff, it's likely to work. People will believe you have an ace or king. *That story makes sense.* They will probably fold a better hand than yours, such as 10♠-10♣, because this flop is better for your range.

Now let's do a reverse.

You raise A♥-K♣.

Flop is 9♦-6♣-5♣.

Can you c-bet bluff?

No – the other players are not going to believe your story. And they are more likely have a hand themselves that connected very strongly with the board.

Earlier in this book I mentioned pro poker player Annette Obrestadt, the young poker pro who won a tournament without looking at her cards (taped over them on her computer screen screen). How'd she do it? A freakishly strong adherence to position and range. She knew to bet flops, turns, and rivers if she had a range advantage. Her stories were so cohesive and plausible it didn't matter what her actual cards were – she could "represent" a hand. Call Disney's corporate office because this woman can make anyone believe in fairytales.

The Range That Beats All Ranges

Raising pre-flop buys you the benefit of a strong range. But it's not the *absolute strongest* – there's no range like a reraise range.

When someone reraises – makes it even more more expensive – they're representing a very narrow range. A-A, K-K, A-K and Q-Q. Certain players won't even reraise the last two.

I *strongly recommend* including pocket jacks and ace-queen into your reraise range. Sometimes pocket nines and tens as well. Don't treat this recommendation like a lifestyle magazine telling you to buy obscure avocado oil or perform lunges in the

supermarket – take this advice seriously. I'm not being ridiculous, I swear.

The benefits of reraising are: make more money on your high-value hands, have the strongest story, take the betting lead, narrow everyone's ranges, get rid of kooky weak hands that could beat you, firmer skin, tighter waistline, more energy in the afternoon, free plane tickets...

Basically, reraising is a really, really good thing.

You're more likely to win the pots you reraised pre-flop *and* for more money/chips.

Limiting your reraise range to A-A and K-K scares people into folding – another reason to reraise more frequently. Every (successful!) poker player these days will mix-up their reraise range with a wide variety of hands to be more unpredictable. But they're doing so as a ploy to imitate the "classic" reraising range.

Tournaments train you to reraise frequently because it's common tourney strategy to "reraise-shove" all your chips.

> **PRO TIP**
> Reraising different types of hands – suited connectors! gappers! – eliminates "range cap." Now your premium range can be wider.

A Tale of Two Stories

A successful poker-playing strategy has more ingredients than your favorite cocktail. And if we were to go over all the of them, it would make you equally dizzy. Too much about stack sizes, equity denial, and combinatorics, and soon you'll be asking the bartender for a double.

Instead let's just get the gist of *general storylines* in poker. No bet sizes. No stack depths. No numbers.

You can always fine-tune and finesse later. Right now, we're setting a foundation.

A Story ...

Jack & **Julia**.

Julia raises K♣-Q♣, and Jack calls with an unknown hand. Mystery!

Flop: A♣-J♣-3♥.

Jack checks, Julia bets, Jack calls.

Turn: A♣-J♣-3♥-7♦.

Julia bets, Jack calls.

River: A♣-J♣-3♥-7♦-7♥.

Julia makes one last bet, and Jack folds the hand J♦-10♦.

Wait, what just happened?

How'd she win? Why'd she keep betting? Why'd Jack fold? Are they destined to be together? Is it true love? Does he have a history of getting caught up with unpredictable women? So many questions!

Julia won the hand not because she had him beat. He had a pair of jacks, and she didn't have anything. But her storyline made sense. He folded assuming she had an ace. Ah, classic tragedy!

But Julia ain't no fool. She wasn't betting blindly, she was *semi-bluffing*. Any club card would make her a flush and any ten would give her a straight. That's called a semi-bluff; bluffing with a draw, when you still have a shot at improving to the winning hand. A hero's or heroine's journey.

Plot Twist

Let's see what happens if we play things a little differently.

Julia raises K♣-Q♣, and Jack calls with his "unknown" hand (no spoilers!).

Flop: A♣-J♣-3♥.

Jack checks, Julia checks because she doesn't have a pair.

Turn: A♣-J♣-3♥-7♦.

Now Jack bets, Julia calls hoping to hit her straight or flush.

River: A♣-J♣-3♥-7♦-7♥.

They both check and Jack scoops the pot with J♦-10♦.

Alternate Ending

In this somber rewrite, Julia is cast as a despondent weak player and loses. They both had the same hands but told different stories. In the first rendition, Julia was a mystery to Jack – maybe she had him beat, maybe she didn't. This time she was passive and predictable – a damsel in distress who never gets saved. Straight to DVD version.

The first time Julia was trying to outplay Jack. The second time she was trying to *outdraw* him. One is drama, the other tragedy.

The Sequel

Jack limps with K♣-Q♣. A new player, Eliza raises. He calls.

Flop: A♣-J♣-3♥.

Jack's been here before – but now the tables are turned!
He checks, Eliza bets, he calls.

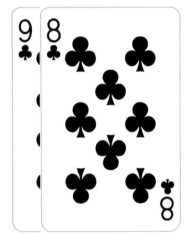

Turn: A♣-J♣-3♥-7♦.

Jack checks, she bets again, he calls.

River: A♣-J♣-3♥-7♦-7♥.

Déjà vu! Neither the flush or straight came. Jack checks, Eliza bets, and he folds, grumbling sarcastically, "nice hand." She reveals 9♣-8♣! Lo and behold, he had her beat!

Jack lost once again because he was afraid to raise. He could've raised pre-flop, or even made a heroic semi-bluff checkraise on the flop (check, then raise). Or he could've bluff-raised the river. Instead he allows his opponents to run over him and receives no love.

A Poker Player with a Past

Poker players who've been around the block play differently. They've been burned before. They're jaded. They've got a chip on their shoulder. They've seen a lot of things happen on the felt and are aware that it's a cruel, cruel world where many hands can beat you.

Here's the set-up: A♣-J♥-3♦-7♠-K♣.

A battle-scared poker veteran will never call flop, turn, and river with a hand like A♠-8♠. Their opponent could have A-Q, two pair, three jacks, three threes, a straight – they've seen it all before. So many hands beat one pair.

Folding is wisdom.

For Better and for Worse

Some people choose chocolate over vanilla[1]. Others choose to put their shoes on before their shirt. Not everyone wants babies. From day-to-day routines to personal philosophies, it's hard to find a unified consensus.

But when you play poker, one desire remains consistent across all parties:

You want worse hands to call and better hands to fold.

That strategy remains the same whether you are playing for pennies or millions. Let's explain our lofty universal truth in real terms.

> The board is 6♣-K♣-4♦-10♣-2♥.
>
> Brad has 6♥-6♠.
>
> Nathan has K♦-J♥.
>
> Does Brad want Nathan to call a bet on the river?
>
> Yes. Duh. Obvi. Brad has a set of sixes (three-of-a-kind), which beats Nathan's single pair of kings. He wants the worse hand to call so he can win the pot. Not a trick question.
>
> Now let's say it's the same board 6♣-K♣-4♦-10♣-2♥
>
> Brad has 6♥-6♠
>
> Anneliese has 8♣-7♣
>
> Does Brad want Anneliese to call a bet on the river? No – her flush beats his set of sixes.

1 My vanilla bean-loving sisters, where you at?

That's fold better, get called by worse at its heart. It sounds easy, but you'd be surprised by how many poker players don't adhere to this mega-important principle.

Folding out all worse and only getting called by better is dubbed a "Game Theory Disaster."

An Example

I was at the final table of a daily poker tournament at a Los Angeles casino in September 2018. Since we were down to the last few players, every time someone was eliminated, there was a pay jump. Those circumstances usually mean the strategy is to play extra straightforward and not get cute raising silly cards. Conservative is cool.

I was first to act and raised. My range here should be two face cards minimum or a big pocket pair. One guy called in the small blind.

The flop was A♣-K♦-Q♠.

Instead of checking to me, he went all-in with K♣-Q♣.

This is terrible! Why?

Because I am only going to call if I have him beat. He is going to fold out everything worse.

Let's say I had raised 9♦-9♥ or J♣-J♦. I now know to fold those hands. And even though it's not fun, I'd probably have to at least consider folding a hand like A♠-J♠ because his story is stronger than one pair. More importantly, if for some frisky reason I had a hand like 5♠-6♠, I'd try to win by bluffing – especially because this flop is perfect for my range. I'm supposed to have lots of aces, kings, and even queens.

But I can't pretend anymore – he took away my ability to bluff!

I can't call a bet with 5♠-6♠, but I could've bluffed with it. And I definitely would've.

He didn't think it through. (On a more human level, he probably just saw his two pair and got excited. Like he went on autopilot!) The "fold better, get called by worse theorem" also serves as a reminder to think before you act. It's a way of slowing down immediate reactions.

Don't Block Someone's Chance to Bluff!

The most common example of this you will see is reraises with top pair. Like so:

Annie raises pre-flop.

Flop: A♦-7♣-3♠.

Annie c-bets.

Sierra reraises with A♣-9♠.

This is a big no-no.

Reraising here with top pair is very bad. Totally amateurish too. An embarrassing mistake, on par with cutting your own bangs as a kid way, way, way above your forehead.

Sierra is only going to get called by better and fold out worse. If Annie was bluffing with a hand like K♣-Q♠ or J♥-10♦, she will fold. There's no way Sierra can earn more chips or money off her; she shut it down. Annie's bluffs are taken away. Even worse, let's say Annie had a hand like A♣-4♦ she'd consider calling bets with. She

now no longer has to wonder. Sierra told her in advance to fold.

That's a disaster. Personal sabotage. A self-inflicted wound. Especially if Annie had a worse ace – because that's how Sierra would make the most money. Annie knows only to continue with two pair, sets, or maybe aces with a very good kicker. A kicker better than Sierra's, that's for sure.

Do not reraise with one pair!

Reraising with one pair inflates the pot!

There are exceptions to every rule – reraising with one pair is appropriate once in a blue moon. I've done it before in choice spots, but only on certain board textures, with a good feel for my opponents. Generally, it's a bad play. If an opponent called your top pair reraise, you're probably going to need to reopen your wallet.

PRO TIP
Good poker is getting max value from worse hands.

Check, Please!

Thanks to darkness we have light, and thanks to check we have bet.

The *art* of checking – choosing not to bet – carries a certain sophistication. A clever check back will elevate your game with elegance, trickery, and finesse.

Reasons to Check #1: Getting Trappy with it

Let's say you have an *amazing* hand and don't want your opponents to know. You can conceal the strength of your hand by *not betting* – a poker strategy called **trapping**. Like asking him where he was last night when you already know.

"Checking the nuts" is common practice in poker.

Common times to check-trap are when you flop *top set* or flop *the nuts* (the best hand possible at that moment). They're so common you should be on the look out when a player unconventionally does this. Alarm bells ringing!

The reason why is because you're so far in the lead, it's difficult for your opponents to have something very valuable. Checking gives them a chance to "catch up."

When you're holding Q♣-Q♠ and the flop is Q♥-Q♦-5♣, there are very few strong hands another player can have (virtually nil) because you know they don't hold a queen. Even someone with pocket rockets (the nickname for two aces) can get worried you have a queen – let alone two of them! Best not to blast them off their hand. Maybe a free turn card will tease them with a straight or flush draw.

PRO TIP

Lightning quick checks are often signs of extreme strength. Most poker players always try to look confident – acting weak is a major red flag.

Flopping top set is a similar scenario. When you have A♣-A♦ and the flop comes 3♦-A♣-7♠, it's hard for someone else to have an ace since there is only one left in the deck. Chances are slim. Everyone sees the ace on the flop loud and clear, which will prompt them to proceed with caution. Here's something funny:

Bluffs can be more convincing if you check. Reverse psychology!

Sometimes I'll actually check to frighten my opponents. Depending on the player, this can be scarier than betting!

Example 1

One time I raised J♣-10♠ in late position and the guy on the button called me. The flop was K♣-K♠-5♣. Obviously I missed the flop; I'd need to win the hand by bluffing.

I decided the most confident-looking thing I could do was check with the plan of betting many turn cards – a club gives me a backdoor flush draw, and any face card improves me to a straight draw or pair. I checked, he checked back. The turn was perfect: 9♣. I bet, he glanced at his cards, clearly thinking, grunted, and folded. Everyone at the table nodded "nice hand" because my play looked spooky strong – and that he was scared to death!

But the reason that worked those times was my story made sense. *Checking nutted hands* is so widely practiced in poker my opponents got the memo.

Reasons to Check #2: Check One, Get One Free

Most times you're not going to flop quads or top set or some other kind of high revenue monster. Sometimes you'll want to check back and see the next card for free.

Someone raises in middle position, you call on the button with 9♠-8♠, and both players in the blinds call. The flop is K♠-8♥-6♦. Each player in the blinds checks (as expected), and the pre-flop raiser also checks. Now the action is on you. What do you do?

Check back here and take a free card. One of the players in the blinds could easily have a king. Checking allows you to see if another eight peels on the turn (or a nine, spade, or straight draw-type card like a seven). See what happens. Embrace the check.

Always check back if you don't want to get raised.

Another good time to check back is if you have a gutshot straight draw or a low pocket pair. The chances of your miracle card coming is low, so you're giving yourself the perfect price: free.

Wouldn't it be nice if you check back a K♥-Q♥-7♦ flop when you raised with A♥-J♥ and the turn card is the 10♥ ? You turned the nuts (straight!) with a redraw to the super nuts (royal flush!) What a gift.

Alternate scenario. You raised pre-flop with 6♥-6♦ . The flop is Q♥-J♥-7♣. Probably a good idea to check back here – especially when the turn card rolls off the beautiful 6♣!

Reasons to Check #3: Control Freak

The last reason to check is for pot control – you don't want to fold, but you don't want to play a huge pot either. Controlling boy-friends are bad. Controlling pots are good.

Poker mastery happens when you can manipulate pots to be as small or big as you want.

Let's say you raised A♦-4♦ and the flop is A♣-5♦-8♠. You very likely have the best hand, but there's no reason to go cra-

PRO TIP

Poker mastery happens when you can manipulate pots to be as small or big as you want.

zy here – if you bet flop, turn, and river, your opponent(s) almost always have you beat. They could have a bigger ace than you, two pair, or a set. Maybe check the flop and bet the turn. Or vice-versa – bet the flop, and check back the turn if there's a caller. You're still building a pot but keeping it much more manageable.

Same deal if you raise J♥-J♠ and the flop is Q♣-6♦-2♠. Many times you will have the best hand here – your opponent may or may not have a queen. Feel free to check here and evaluate on the turn if you think your cards are winning.

Even better, your opponents might (wrongly!) interpret your check as weakness, calling any future bets with a worse holding like a pair of tens or sevens. Checking for *pot control* helps you get called by worse hands.

> **Checking can be a sign of a medium strength hand like a midsize pocket pair or top pair with a weak kicker.**
>
> **If you're worried you'll only get called by a better hand, consider checking with the intention of *bluff-catching*.**

Check Like the Cool Kids

Most rushes in poker come from pulling a big bluff or making a great call. But I'll never forget the first time I made a clever check.

I raised pre-flop from early/middle position with A♠-K♦. One player called from the small blind.

The flop was J♣-2♥-7♣. He checked to me. I decided to c-bet, and he called.

Turn was A♦.

He checked.

My autopilot excitement kicked in – I'd hit my card! Natural instinct told me to bet.

114

But I'd just watched a poker video on YouTube (Jamie Gold vs Prahlad Friedman) from the 2006 World Series of Poker Main Event which had given me inspiration. I wanted to play in the Main Event too!

In the WSOP hand, Jamie raised K♦-10♦. Prahlad called out of the big blind with 7♦-7♣. Flop: 4♦-2♣-2♠. Jamie bet, Prahlad called. Turn: A♠. Prahlad checked again, Jamie checked back. River: 3♣. Prahlad checks his pair of sevens, and Jamie bluff-bets with his king-high.

"You hit that ace on the turn, didn't you?" asks Prahlad, talking himself into a fold.

Obviously, Jamie didn't hit the ace – but that didn't matter. If he had hit the ace, what a cool play that would've been, I thought to myself. I wanted to be someone who was capable of that. I wanted to be someone who could check an ace back on the turn. I wanted to be someone who made the pros squirm.

So I checked back my ace. Thanks, Prahlad.

The river was an offsuit low number card. My opponent led into me with a big bet, and I comfortably called.

He was shocked I called. Clearly wasn't expecting that! He embarrassedly turned over K♣-Q♠. (When I flipped over my hand after, the guy next to me with the biggest stack at the table said, "well played!")

I adhered to poker's golden rule alive: fold out better, get called by worse. On that turn card, I'm rarely getting called by a worse hand – he may have two pair, like ace-jack, a set, or a high equity hand like A♣-10♣ – say he flopped the flush draw and picked up the ace – which means he may shove on me/go all-in if I bet the turn. I liked my hand, but one pair is not good enough to call a fat raise. Checking the turn in this spot is textbook pot control.

By checking the turn, it's also more likely I get paid on the river by a jack and bluff-catch busted flush draws. Or busted pair draws, like K♣-Q♠.

Amanda's Advice

Throughout this chapter, I explained how checking is a sign of strength. And also weakness. And also something in the middle. Which is it?

The truth is, elegant poker incorporates all three.

Elite players can tell a tale in tandem with the community cards. Checking on some boards looks crazy confident. Other times it looks wimpish and mouse-like. Every time you check tells your opponent something about the strength of your hand – the art is in getting them to think what you want them to think.

Certain people always view checking as weakness and only respect big bets. (These are usually amateurs or beginners.) For others, checking is more suspect.

Graceful poker involves adapting to various player types and scenarios. Versatility is the secret behind any sophisticated strategy; rigidity is predictable and easily abused. Think of poker as a microcosm for life: Don't rely on the same maneuvers. Doing the same thing every time is bad battlefield strategy, and saying the same thing to every guy is bad date strategy. Success in war, love, and cards entails the power of reception – because it puts you in position for a little deception.

No More Half-baked Bets!

I'm majorly guilty of half-baked ideas. Starting a new blog, band, or book... not all business plans are good ones!

And neither are too many half-pot bets.

It's true that standard c-bet sizing is half pot. But the more advanced your poker game becomes, the more you will want to fine-tune. Welcome to bet-sizing 202.

Go Big or Go Home

If your stack size is huge, your opponents may fold to you out of fear – they don't want to be in a decision for so many chips. Big stack bullying! Especially in tournaments.

Fold equity *refers to your chances of making your opponent fold.*

It's a semi-bluff, and especially useful when playing draws.

Even with a fantastic flush draw or straight draw, you still don't have a showdownable hand – one measly pair beats you.

Never bet with your draws unless you have some presumed fold equity (for if you don't hit).

First we need to decide if we're going to bet the turn. 9♦-8♦-K♠ is a fine flop to bet Q♦-10♦. You can keep keep betting the turn, repping a king if your flush draw (or gutshot straight draw!) doesn't come through, or win a big pot if it does. Betting here will keep 'em guessing.

But continuing to bet a Q♦-10♦ flush draw on the turn after 4♦-J♦-J♠ flop isn't always smart because if your opponent has a jack, they're never folding. The semi-bluff won't work.

So we're looking to play turn cards…

You're in that same situation with Q♦-10♦ and the flop is 9♦-8♦-K♠. You bet the flop, and were called by one player. They check to you on a brick turn.

Now what?

Option a) Bet – continue building the pot and applying pressure to one-pair hands.

Option b) Check – take a free card and see if you hit the river cheaply.

Either choice is a winner. They're both right answers. That said, if you bet, I suggest you bet big. What you don't want to do is bet small. That encourages single pair hands to come along for the ride. Avoid easy-to-call small or midsize bets. "Not too hot, not too cold" is as lame as it sounds.

Example

This hand was taken from an online tournament.

Bridget raises in late position with 8♣-7♣.

Player on the button calls. Cindy calls in the big blind.

Flop: 5♠-8♦-10♣

Cindy checks. Bridget bets. Player on the button folds. Cindy calls.

Turn: 5♠-8♦-10♣-6♣

What a turn card! Bridget turns a flush draw AND open-ended straight draw to go with her pair of eights.

What should she do?

She can always play it safe and check. Or she can bet. Either way is fine, but if she bets, she shouldn't bet small here – Her opponent will almost certainly call a small or medium-sized bet with a hand like a ten. And if the last card doesn't improve her holding, she's a bit stuck.

River 1: 5♠-8♦-10♣-6♣-2♥

If Bridget had bet with a moderate sizing on the turn, encouraging a ten to stick around, then she will have a hard time getting Cindy to fold to any bet on this river. Now she's in an awkward spot with a lousy pair of eights. She inflated the pot, and is in a bloated scenario worse than trying to squeeze into skinny jeans after a night of binging on nachos. Bleh.

That's why she needed to bet big. Cindy folding would still be a victory.

If Bridget does get called, the times she hits, she'll make the max. Another problem she's facing is that all rivers that make her hand are scare cards – they spook people into folding.

River 2: 5♠-8♦-10♣-6♣-4♣

That's a very scary river card for Cindy to call a bet with just a ten.

When it comes to betting a draw, go big!

Any seven makes a straight. There's also a backdoor flush which completed and some likely two pairs. Bridget will have hit this river, but won't get paid.

That's why Bridget decided a girl's gotta do what a girl's gotta do.

She went all-in on the turn. Cindy tanked and *tanked* ("thought and thought!") before finally finding a fold. Did she make the right choice? We'll never know – the beauty of the move.

If Cindy had a hand like K♣-10♦, then she has a 57% chance of winning after the turn card versus Bridget's 43% chance.

There is also a chance Cindy didn't have a ten. She may have called the flop with an open-ended straight draw such as J♠-9♥ or 7♣-6♣ (which would have turned a pair of sixes). A small bet might inspire her to continue and then bluff Bridget on the river if she misses.

PRO TIP

Betting big on semi-bluffs will make it more likely for your opponents to call you when you're not bluffing. Mix it up!

Tournament Time

There comes a time in every poker player's life when he or she enters a tournament. Or, as Winston Churchill said: "To every man[1] there comes in his lifetime that special moment when he is figu-

ratively tapped on the shoulder and offered a chance to do a very special thing, unique to him and fitted to his talents. What a tragedy if that moment finds him unprepared or unqualified for the work which would be his finest hour" – if we're going to get all deep and mythological about it (cue the orchestra!), live life romantically.

Tournaments have all the glory, prestige, prizes. No one ever got famous playing at their cousin's house on New Year's. When you play a regular poker game at a casino – a "cash game" – the most notoriety you'll ever receive is a kind nod partnered with "well played."

First Time

My first tournament had about 90 players, and I was the 2nd person eliminated (largely because I got into this bluff-reraise war on the river with nothing – whoops!) Sullen and heartbroken, I debated a re-entry. All the guys at the table kept trying to convince me – they wanted to take all my chips.

Except one guy.

---

1 Or woman...!

He'd been bragging about all his final table wins, and looked me straight in the eye before saying: "You're bad at tournaments."

I did re-enter and, seven hours later, him and I were the final two.

He kept trying to make all these chop deals that were extremely in his favor (a "chop" means splitting the winnings right then and there instead of playing until elimination – with the bigger stacked player taking a larger cut). I told him it was my first tournament, I never expected to make it the final table, no deal.

> My opponent first proposed a chop deal when we were 3-handed. He was the big stack, I was middle, and the other player was a teeny-tiny short stack with near nothing. If we played all played it through, first place would receive around $2,200, second place $1,300, and third place $1,100. He gobsmackingly suggested him taking $2,000, with the other player and I *both* taking $1,300. Some nerve!

That's how I won my first tournament.

I won a huge pot going all-in on the river as a bluff, and busted him the next hand. First place prize money paid in full!

What is a Tournament?

Poker tournaments have eliminations. Cash games do not.

What happens if you lose all your chips in a cash game? You can buy more (bank account permitting). Unlimited entry.

Tournaments play down to the last men and women standing – when you're out, you're out. Sometimes a tournament will allow you to re-enter near the beginning (usually the first two hoursish). But after a certain point, your *tournament life* will be on the line. No more chances.

Most tournaments pay the top 10 percent. If 100 people entered, 10 people would win money.

To accelerate the elimination process, *the blinds increase* – it will become increasingly more expensive to play. Let's say you start with 30,000 chips and the blinds are 50/100. Super cool! Awesome! You could do this forever. Until the blinds rev up to 5,000/10,000 – now you to have to commit nearly your entire stack just to see a flop.

Plus there's an ante – an extra amount either everyone or the person sitting in the big blind will have to pay. That makes each pot exceptionally lucrative and worth fighting for, both because there's more chips to be won and more consequence for not playing hands. You can comfortably fold every hand in a cash game if you want to and sit at the table for several hours. If you fold every hand in a tournament, the blinds and antes will eat away at you until you have no chips left – getting *"blinded out".*

Tournaments usually last several hours, and sometimes days.

Since the money for a tournament is pooled – although the casino still takes a portion from each person's entry fee – you can win much greater amounts. It's the most feasibly way to go from $200 to $2,000 in one sitting.

Tournaments have more short-term swings ("variance"). When the blinds are steep, skill matters much less – there isn't anything a pro can do with just a few big blinds. All-in or fold. For this reason, *tournaments are much more beginner-friendly. Luck plays a bigger role*, and winning a tournament requires serious run good[2]. Hot streaks can't be taught.

PRO TIP

Folding too much in a tournament will cause the blinds and antes to eat away at your stack. **Do not let this happen.**

---

2 Catching premium cards, winning hands, getting lucky.

Stack Size Strategery[3]

Increasing blinds means stack sizes matter more – you don't want to play a pretty hand like 9♠-8♠ with less than 10 big blinds. If you miss the flop – which will happen 2/3 times – you can't scare your opponents by bluffing since most of your chips are already in the middle.

> ## Tournament Golden Rule
> **The chips you lose are more important than the chips you gain. *Girl's Guide* version: "every chip counts."**

The classic tournament adage is "the chips you lose are more important than the chips you gain." A simpler way of thinking about this is **"every chips counts"**. The size of your stack changes which cards you play, so it's best not to leak chips.

Shove It!

When you enter a tournament, be prepared there's a good chance you'll need to shove – go all-in – before the flop. It's the fastest and easiest way to earn chips. If everyone folds, congrats, the blinds and antes go to you (free money!)

PRO TIP
Don't commit more than 1/3 of your stack without going all-in pre-flop.

> ## Steal My Heart
> **Shoving pre-flop to scare everyone away and win the chips uncontested is called a "steal."**

"Stealing" by shoving pre-flop is an especially aggressive way to build your stack – winning by forcing everyone to fold. Think of it as bluffing pre-flop. Qui Nguyen won $8,005,310 in the 2016 Main

---

3 Shout-out to those who watch *Saturday Night Live*.

Event; on one hand he went all-in pre-flop with 8♠-5♥. Did he want to get called? No – of course not! He wanted to win the blinds and antes for free by making everyone think he had a big hand like pocket aces or kings.

Stealing only works when you have "fold equity" – enough chips to scare someone into folding.

You need a better hand to call with than to shove. Qui can shove with 8♠-5♥ as a bluff, but he can't call someone else's shove with that hand for value. In tournaments, you generally want to shove wide but call tight. Don't be afraid to put people to the test for a huge amount of chips – it's perfectly reasonable to go all-in pre-flop with a hand like A♦-J♣. But you usually don't want to call someone's shove with that hand. You are flipping against most pairs, and you're crushed by bigger aces.

It's easier to shove than call a shove.

When it's folded around to the last few people, it's common for people to shove very wide from the button or small blind. I've shoved with all sorts of hands from those positions (especially blind on blind). Since you only have to beat one or two players, your steal is much more likely to work.

PRO TIP

20 big blinds is a perfect reraise "shove stack" size because the chips gained will be significant, but people will also be afraid to call you.

There are several push/fold charts and apps to train you which cards to shove and when (see mine on amandasaces.com!). Some of the results may surprise you. Play around with them. Practice your shove game. Just don't forget to consider your opponents. Some will be more inclined to call than others – they don't care what the chart says!

Bluff Up the Power!

When you play a cash game, you don't have to bluff. Your win rate will be smaller, but you could comfortably take your time, patiently wait for the very best cards, and only bet when you're a near certain winner. Easy game[4].

Tournaments are not so – you must bluff. There's pressure to win pots – *quick! quick! quick!* before the blinds go up! – meaning there's pressure to make moves. Can't hit the board? Figure it out. You can't wait until K♥-Q♦ flops a straight.

Which also means your opponents have more incentive to bluff.

But wait. There's more.

Bluffing is different in tournaments. Way different. Because it's more important that you're right.

Make a bad call in a cash game? It's OK – you can always buy more chips. Make a bad call in a tournament? Now you may have been playing for several hours only to cripple your stack trying to be a hero. Curiosity killed the cat.

Tournaments have fewer "curiosity calls" and less "I just want to see what you have." Since there is much more *risk* in making the wrong read, the psychology changes. You can apply more pressure knowing your opponents must be dead sure – their tournament life is on the line.

---

4 Kinda.

Bubble Bullies

The tensest time in a tournament is nearly always *the bubble* – the cutoff for who gets paid and who doesn't. Let's say the top 10 earn prize money, and everyone else walks away with nothing. You certainly don't want to place 11th!

Same goes for massive pay jumps.

Take the 2018 WSOP Main Event for example (entry fee $10,000; and 7,874 people entered). The difference between 7th and 8th place was $250,000. But the jump between 2nd and 3rd was $1,250,000 – that's more than a *million dollar difference(!)*.

A million dollars to me may not be the same as a million dollars to you which may not be the same as a million to dollars to, say, Taylor Swift (unless of course you are Taylor Swift, in which case, *"heyyy! Don't you worry your pretty little mind, people throw rocks at things that shine!"* Please write a country song about cards).

How much do you care about money?

Pressure

The most intense money pressure spot I ever experienced was in a $365 entry tournament in October 2017[5]. There were more than 656 entrants, and we were down to the last three tables (final 20 or so remaining). First prize was a hair under $40,000 (something like $39,987). Getting knocked out right then in 20xth place was for around $1,300. If everyone were to split the prize pool equally, we would all receive about $7,000 each.

I was the tournament chipleader for most of the event[6]. By this time, I had dropped from biggest stack in the room to probably 2nd in chips – still a tremendous advantage over the rest of the field.

5 Junkies Poker Open.
6 Tournament buy-in was for 15,000 chips. At one point, I had more than 800,000 – making me by far the biggest stack in the room.

A GIRL'S GUIDE TO POKER

There was only one man at my table who had me "covered" (had a bigger stack than me). He was a youngish-looking guy in his early thirties with scruffy hair and sunglasses – like if Shaggy from *Scooby-Doo!* played poker. And even though he had a huge stack, he was pushing a chop. He wanted everyone to split the money and just take their 7 grand, no contest. I didn't know what do – this was barely my sixth month playing poker and I never expected to be put in such a position. I texted my dad for advice. He said if I was one of the biggest stacks – which I very obviously was – then I should wait until we're down to the final table and split the money then. Ok, sounds good.

Then this hand happened:

Chipleader/Shaggy from *Scooby-Doo!* raised from early position.

I was on the button with 9♣-9♦.

This is a spot I'd usually 3-bet (reraise). But I looked over at the guy in the big blind, who had been at my table prior, and was a bit of a maniac. He was getting short-stacked – I figured if I flatted with my nines, he would shove as a steal – *no matter what cards he had*. Given this, I decided to just call with my nines, planning on getting all-in with him.

Like clockwork, when it was his turn, he went all-in. (For the record here, he had 8♣-5♥; I had a stone-cold read. My plan was working perfectly.)

The chipleader asked for a count, thought about it, then called.

Now I went all-in as an isolation play (pocket nines are much more likely to win against one opponent than two.)

Shaggy chipleader man tanked and tanked and tanked – thought about it *forever*. After around two minutes, someone called "clock" on him (time-limited his decision because he was taking so long). At this point, I was thinking my nines were good – maybe he didn't want to flip against me with a hand like A♣-Q♠ or something. He looked so distressed – and there was no point in bluffing now, he was genuinely troubled – I thought perhaps I even wanted a call.)

Then he finally says, "I'm sorry, I have to call you, I have aces."

130

"ACES?!" I said in shock (as did everyone watching from the side-lines – we were all flabbergasted!)

I flopped a gutshot draw but didn't hit. 8♣-5♥ rivered a straight, and that was that. I was out. A commanding chipstack to getting a little more than my money back. They chopped around an hour later at the final table for 10 grand per person. I had so many chips I literally could've folded my way to $10,000.

I thought about his decision for a while. At first, it seems crazy – pre-flop he knows he's winning. Doesn't matter what I have. He's always an 80% favorite, give or take a per-centage point or two.

But *I was the only person who was truly a threat to him* – he had me covered by just a few blinds. And while 80% of the time he wins, 20% of the time he loses. He has $365 invested. If he calls me then with his aces, he figures eight out of ten times he wins anywhere between $7,000 and $40,000, and the other 20% of the time he walks away with relatively nothing[7].

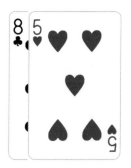

That's what we call pressure.

How much?

What price point is too much for you to risk? Would you risk $100 as an 80% favorite? What about $1,000? $10,000?

---

7 The flop was 10♥-6♣-7♦, meaning any eight or nine would've indeed made me the win-ner (25%). (River was a 4♥, which gave 8♣-5♥ the straight.) One out of every four (25%) times precludes himself from winning $7,000-$40,000 and he only has $365 invested.

So You Think You Can Bluff?

Good girls can go bad, and good bluffs can go wrong.

Since poker is all about telling a story, good bluffers tell convincing tales – unlike that fair-weather friend or new flame who can't get back to you because they "never check their phone" and "just aren't big on texting." Cool story bro. Tell it again.

What makes a good poker story?

The underlying theme of any poker story is *table image.*

Table image is how other players see you.

Do they think you are a maniac player pulling fast ones – a real life Blufferella? Or do they think you are a sweet little fawn who only bets when she has it? People won't solely be judging the believability of your bluff. *They'll judge the believability coming from you.*

Stereotypes say women play conservatively.

All the time I am asked what's it like to be a woman playing poker.

Stereotypes say women only raise big pairs and face cards. Guys have made crazy laydowns to me pre-flop – folding pocket tens, jacks, and even kings to me face-up! (Every time they were wrong – I almost always had ace-queen)! The truth is you should rarely ever limp in Texas Hold 'Em; I regularly raise hands like pocket fours and 7-6 suited.

But for some reason pre-flop men always put me on ace-king.

And post-flop, they still always put me on ace-king!

♦ Girls playing poker are perceived as tight pre-flop, and loose/passive post-flop.

♦ Some guys set out subconsciously to play big pots against girls, treating it as a battle of the sexes.

When it comes to table image, it takes two to tango – *pay attention to whom you're bluffing*. Some people are more bluffable than others. The more money someone has, the more they can afford to call for kicks and giggles. Since seeing a woman playing poker is a novelty, you'll also have people calling you light sometimes just to see what kind of cards you play. Curiosity kills the cat. Or your nice bluff spot. *Be conscious of people who will call your bets for amusement.* (Remember that many, many people will cling to you always having ace-king! There may be no convincing them otherwise. No matter how well you executed your semi-bluff triple-barrel!)

The best time to take advantage of female stereotypes is in small tournaments. Beating the daily tourneys at most casinos involves going all-in pre-flop at times to "steal" the blinds and antes (translation: free money). Since you will most likely be perceived as tighter pre-flop, you can shove a wider range of hands and generate folds.

Light Calldown

A perfect example of a light calldown happened between me and another woman. I was in a daily poker tournament at a Los Angeles casino, and we were one elimination away from being at the final table.

A few people limped, and I put in a big raise out of the small blind with 8♣-8♠. Sort of a "squeezeplay.[1]" The woman limp-called from early position. Everyone else folded. We were off to a flop!

Flop: 3♦-8♥-10♥

I checked (praying she had something), she bet, I called.

Turn: 4♦

I checked, she bet, I raised – extremely aggressive. She called.

River: 10♥

Dream card! I rivered a full house and jammed all-in.

She thought and thought about it, and finally said, "I don't think you have any of that!" The woman called for nearly her entire stack – with ace-high. Even someone like her who plays day in and day out and does reasonably well (I have seen her before at final tables) was

---

1 A squeeze play is a reraise to a very large size to steal the pot. This example was not a reraise, but since so many people limped I sized it like a bluffy squeezeplay trying to take the pot down uncontested.

unaccustomed to a girl raising a medium pocket pair like 8♣-8♠[2]. Completely bewildered.

That time worked out in my favor – which doesn't always happen.

Very, Very Light Calldown

January 2017, I entered a $550 tournament at the Los Angeles Poker Classic. This wasn't a regular poker daily.

I was terribly, terribly card dead, and in the span of 2-3 hours, only raised one or two hands. No reraises.

Finally, I found my moment. The under-the-gun player was a loose guy who raised every hand (which he did again). There were several callers (a good three or four people).

I looked down at my hand in the small blind: K♠-Q♠. Again, a good spot for a squeeze – I put in a hefty reraise. My first reraise yet.

---

2 Remember that most women are perceived as very tight pre-flop, incapable of raising a hand like 8♣-8♠. That is why my story did not make sense to this very regular player.

Only the UTG player called. Off to a flop!

Flop: J♣-3♣-10♠.

Not bad! I had an open-ended straight draw with two overcards. Even if I was up against a set of jacks or an overpair like aces I had outs to win. I c-bet 1/3 of my stack – planning to shove any turn card.

He called.

Turn: 6♣

Not the greatest turn card – a flush beats me – but I was committed at this point. I went all-in shoving for an almost exact pot-sized bet. This was for over half his stack as well.

He snap-called. Didn't ask for a count. Didn't have to think about it. Tossed in a single chip to call confidently assuming his hand was good.

I reluctantly flipped over my hand, and he turned over his: 6♠-4♠. He had hit the six. And since in his eyes it was impossible for me to have anything other than ace-king, he figured his "pair draw" was good. (And no, I did not hit the river – busted out of the tournament).

I suspect this was also a "curiosity call" since I had hardly played any hands – the assumption he had made was that I only play one; ace-king.

Expect an insane number of people to rigidly put you on ace-king because your table image is half the story, not just the bets.

Adjust
Compensate by creating mega pots with your value hands.

She's Got the Look

Guy, girl, tall, short, fat, or thin – tailoring your image is a poker table essential. You're going to want to know how people see you. And use it! If looks could ~~kill~~ pay.

A timid or serious aesthetic gets more credit. Other players will doubt you're bluffing – which means you should do more of it! Play "small ball" little pots with minor bluffs and they're likely to get through; people will give you the benefit of the doubt (e.g. they'll likely fold a pair of nines to you on a A♣-8♦-5♥ flop; at least if you bet the turn) You'll grind out a modest profit without having to make many big decisions for huge amounts of chips.

Then there's the wildcard image, the "does she have it, does she not?" If people think you're messing around and pulling moves on them, be prepared: you will get called! So you lose a few medium pots here and there.

When you really have it, you'll win massive. Unpredictability is the way to be the most profitable in poker – albeit the swingiest.

Keep your eyes open for people trying to make you see them a certain way – drunk, gambling, or lil Miss Clueless. A lot of times it's a *hustle*. Some sharks will purposely turn over junky cards as *"free advertising"* – don't fall for it. They're spewing a few bucks at the beginning so you'll pay them off big later.

Alcohol is also used as a prop and façade. Poker players act drunk (or, okay, are drunk) hoping you'll think they don't know what they're doing.

They know exactly what they're doing.

When I was playing at the Wynn in Vegas, we ordered a round of drinks for the table. Then I got into a hand against another girl. She clearly knew how to play, but also came across as super-serious. (Uptight, much?)

I opened pocket tens and flopped quads. (the board was 10♠-10♥-7♣-7♦-J♠). The good news was that I couldn't be beaten. Bad news was that it's highly unlikely for her to have anything of value (since I know she doesn't have a ten). By the river card, the pot was small: $40. This was a problem. I knew if I got too fancy with a checkraise or bet any reasonable size she'd see right through it; standard poker was against me. Instead I emphasized my intoxicated flair, and said in my whiniest, highest, annoyingest I'm-drunk-and-dumb-and-have-no-idea-what-I'm-doing tone of voice: "I think I have a better hand than you!" and *bombed* it[3] on the river for $400. She thought I was ridiculous, a boozy beginner. She made the call[4]. I turned over my cards and we both sobered up instantly.

> **Poker isn't just numbers – it's psychology. Play accordingly.**

---

3 Major bet.
4 She never showed what she had.

Pressure Cooker

Good bluffs apply incredible pressure – they've gotta put your opponent in a tough spot. The most elegantly sized bets and artful adherence to *board texture* (what the flop, turn, and river look like) totally go out the window if it's too cheap to call. Poker is a game. People play for fun – one of the most exciting things to do is catch someone with their pants down. Second only to bluffing.

Don't believe everything you see on TV. Poker pros bluff *way more* because there is more money on the line[5] – *a $200,000 pot is very different from a $200 pot*. Micro-stakes games make it very, very hard to bluff because there is little you can do to make someone truly squirm. They'll call if they think they're right most of the time (more or less). Or just enough of the time. When making calls for thousands, hundreds of thousands, and even millions of dollars, the average person is going to want to be right much more often than 50/50.

Can't Take the Heat

Poker pros will lay down huge hands on the flop or turn when the pressure is turned high. Art Papazyan astonishingly folded to a single bet on the turn not wanting to risk $60,000 with bottom set, and Maria Ho famously tossed a set of tens on the flop during the 2017 World Series of Poker Main Event. When interviewed, she said she figured she was a roughly 65% favorite (true) – too small a percentage for her taste when a big tournament title on the line.

Pressure is higher in tournaments than cash games because once you're eliminated, you're eliminated – you can't just reach into your pocket and buy more chips. *That means there is greater demand to be right – and thus more incentive to bluff.*

---

5 Plus they also want to look cool on camera.

Bluff-catching

One-pair hands are classic *bluff-catchers* – they can't beat any strong value hands, but they can beat a bluff. Calling someone's bet with ace-high or x-high is calling down with nothing – but saying *my* nothing beats *your* nothing. Welcome to teenage break-ups.

If the run-out was 7♦-8♦-4♦-3♣-9♥ and I called a river-bet with A♣-A♠, I am not beating any value hands – two pair, straight, set, flush – just bluffs. Because players with a feel for the game would never bet a hand like A♦-8♣ on the river hoping to get called; they're only getting called by better.

That's why it's important not to get married to big pocket pairs like aces, kings, or queens. Although they are usually the best hand, *it's uncommon for someone to bet aggressively with anything less valuable than one pair.* By the river, they are virtually bluff-catchers.

What constitutes as a bluff-catcher will vary by board. Sometimes all you need is a single pair or high card. Other times even a hand as strong as two pair or a set is a bluff-catcher. (e.g. K♥-Q♥ is a bluff-catcher on a A♠-K♠-Q♦-3♠-9♥ board)

Getting Caught

Bluffing is tricky for beginners because you need to understand *relative* hand strength . Sometimes a pair of aces is strong. Sometimes it's weak.

Bluff-Catching with Ace-High

One of the most exhilarating things to do in poker is calling a bluff without a pair – just ace-high!

> Women usually are given more situations to bluff-catch with a high card. I can't tell you how many times I've called correctly with ace-high, king-high, and even queen-high. *Because as a girl, you are more likely to get bluffed.* But I've heard guys my same age complain about how they can never make a single accurate ace-high call. My personal theory is that it's because there are less opportunities – people don't want to bluff a young 25-year-old dude.

Here's an example. Our tournament table had just started and we were short-handed (only five players). Short-handed play is more aggressive, so I raised A♦-7♠ under the gun.

The guy on the button called and so did the man in the small blind.

Flop: K♣-Q♠-2♦.

This flop is about as bad as it gets – which is why it's terrible to raise a hand like A♦-7♠! It's very likely my opponents hit the king or queen or maybe even a two. And let's say I was ahead – they called with a hand like J♥-10♦ – they're going to call my flop bet with their straight draw and could easily bluff me on the river. Bad hand. Bad situation. (There isn't really any flop you want to see with ace-seven that doesn't involve multiple sevens).

Gentleman in the small blind checked to me. I decided to give up and check. Guy on the button checked as well.

Turn: 8♠

Small blind checked, I checked, and button bet.

Man in the small blind folded – had he called, I would've ran away faster than Taylor Lautner's[6] acting career.

An eight is a very weird card to bet on – why would he bet with an eight? The small blind or myself – especially the small blind[7] – could easily have at least a queen. On a co-ordinated board with many likely pairs and straight draws, it wouldn't have made sense for the guy on the button to checkback a king – he was repping a queen or nothing. Unless he turned a set of eights. That would make sense.

Still, his sizing seemed peculiar for a set of eights, and my general read was that ace-high could've been good. I made the call.

River: 5♦

I checked, he bet again. The five is a really weird card to bet – what's he trying to rep? He should never be betting an eight or five for value. And I didn't think there was any reason to checkback a king or really even a queen on the flop. The whole thing seemed fishy to me: if my ace-high was good on the turn, it was good on the river as well – the five didn't improve any hands which weren't already beating me.

I made the call; he said "good call" and went to muck. But I had to see his hand. He said "you're good," and, finally, he showed A♠-3♣. My ace-high had him out-kicked.

---

6 The stud from *Twilight*.

7 He's more likely to have a queen than I am because I am betting most of my queens on either flop or turn, but he may very likely check both times.

Takeaways

1) This is bluff-catching in its purest form. My hand only beats a bluff; I can't win against anything he's *trying* to get called by.

2) Good bluffers tell good stories. His story didn't add up – I didn't think he'd checkback a king or queen on the flop, and he shouldn't be betting a low pair like an eight for value. Those hands would usually checkback river and pray they win.

Change of Plans

They say you are the company you keep. If your goal is to be wealthy and rich, find a man with a plan (or a lady with a Mercedes!) The best poker players are good at making plans. (Easy example: you flop a flush draw – what are you going to do if you don't hit your flush on the turn? Think ahead.)

And they also can adjust to plans. Sometimes you concoct a brilliant plan on the flop to bluff, barrel[8], or trap, and then the next card ruins everything. Like you were going to sucker your opponent in and checkraise the turn when you have 7♦-3♣ and the flop is A♥-7♠-3♦, but the turn is A♣. Whoops – back to the drawing board. Time for a new plan (most likely give up).

PRO TIP

Your ability to think two steps ahead and make quick pivots will determine how good you can really get.

Max skill level.

---

8 Riddle Me This: All barrels are bluffs, but not all bluffs are barrels.

A common "change of plans" scenario is when someone has a big pocket pair such as A♥-A♣ or K♣-K♠. Since they know they have their opponent beat pre-flop, the plan is usually bet, bet, bet on the flop, turn, and river. But what if the runout is 5♠-6♠-7♥-8♠-10♦? Almost always pocket aces or kings are beat here. Abort mission!

When you're thinking about what's next in poker, ask yourself this on each card: *did the board change?* Meaning is the hand that was winning on the flop still winning, or is it more likely the other player's hand improved – giving them the lead?

Try It Yourself!

Flop: J♠-10♠-4♥

Turn: A♠

Did the turn card change anything?

a) Yes.

b) No.

The answer is a) Yes!

That turn card changed everything – the obvious flush draw came in, as did the open-ended straight draw (king-queen now has a straight). A pair of jacks or tens now loses to someone's pair of aces. So if your K♦-K♣ was winning on the flop, it's probably not on the turn.

Always think! Did the last card change anything?

Hindsight is 20/20, and if only we had thought things through.

All the time in poker people simply forget to think (guilty as charged!)

Inducing a Bluff

Earlier in this chapter I mention an amateur player (see bluff-catching on page 140) — a mistakes-making prototype if I ever saw one. Amateur, Exhibit A. A few hands prior in that tournament, we got caught in a hand together.

He raised late position, I called from the button with K♣-Q♥.

Flop was K♠-3♥-2♣. He checked, and I checked back as a trap — I knew he didn't have anything, most likely an ace-high hand, and decided to risk allowing an ace to peel off on the turn.

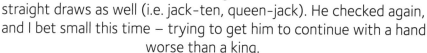

Turn: 9♣

This is what's considered a *wet* turn card — now there are a number of draws. The obvious club flush draw, and a few gutshot straight draws as well (i.e. jack-ten, queen-jack). He checked again, and I bet small this time — trying to get him to continue with a hand worse than a king.

He hesitated and called with something sub-par (not a very good actor).

River: 7 ♥

All of a sudden he bets big. More than I was expecting, but it was still an easy call for me, all things considered. He shook his head and reluctantly turned over A♠-Q♠ — exactly the kind of hand I expected.

On the tournament break, he told me he played that hand terribly; he called me on the turn because he thought I picked up a draw and was semi-bluffing. He also said he didn't think I had a king (that's the idea).

I said I didn't fault him for the turn play – maybe I *was* bluffing with a draw. His ace-high could've been good.

So he drummed up a plan: bluff-catch with ace-high.

That is absolutely fine. In this particular case he was wrong (trapped!), but it's an understandable idea.

The problem is that the river didn't change anything, but he did – now this guy turned his hand into a bluff! If I *was* betting into a draw with queen-jack or jack-ten or some lower suited club cards, those hands are still losing to him (save for something like 8-7 of clubs). If he was beating those hands on the turn, he's still beating those hands on the river. So why the big bet? As the adage goes: he's only getting better hands to call and worse hands to fold. Game theory disaster.

Truth be told, if he checked, I would've value-bet my king – but for a lot cheaper. He could've bluff-caught me at a far less expensive price. Instead he lost the maximum.

When I tried talking to him about it at the break, it was like explaining budgeting to a 20-year-old – not interested! I ran into him a few days later at a cash game and stacked him in an easily avoidable spot[9]. Some people never learn!

---

9 Huge beginner mistake: calling big pre-flop reraises with suited aces. I reraised with Q-Q and he called with A♠-3♠. Loss was completely unnecessary!

Favorite Bluff Battle

My favorite bluff battle took place May 2018 in a poker tournament at the Hustler Casino in Los Angeles. (This was also my first time playing a poker tournament with my dad – I wanted to make him proud!)

We were down to the last men standing – plus me! Final five. (My dad had already been eliminated unfortunately, so it was up to me to carry the family honor.)

The tournament cost $130 to enter, first place received over $1,000, and 5th received about $200 (total). The pay jumps between 1st-5th were huge; we discussed a "chop" by stack size. Biggest stack would get the most and smallest would get the least. Payouts ranged between $500 and $950. I was the second biggest stack and agreed to the deal.

There was only one player who didn't want to chop: an adorable Backstreet Boy-styled guy who looked like he just turned 21 yesterday. He was the table *short stack* – he had the least amount of chips – so a chop deal would've benefited him most. He refused, so we kept on playing.

I raised K♠-J♥ under-the-gun (not really since we were only five-handed). He defended his big blind, and we were heads-up to the flop! Backstreet Boy, quit playing games with my heart (cards!)

Flop: 9♦-7♥-2♦

Ugh – probably one of the worst flops possible. Extremely favors his range; he checked, and I'd usually check here. But he was short-stacked so I decided to bet to apply pressure. He called.

Turn: 2♠

Backstreet Boy shoves all-in. Just open bombs it right into me.

Now a major leak in my game is I make decisions too quickly. But I decided to take my time with this one and *asked the dealer for a count* of his chips[10] – if I called and he won, then he and I would switch places. I'd be the short stack.

Plus there was the real problem: I had nothing. No pair, no draw, just naked king-high.

But his story didn't make any sense.

What exactly was he representing? He shouldn't have any deuces in his range because he was calling a raise pre-flop with not too many chips – and, even if he did, he probably wouldn't have gone all-in. Would've tried to trap. Same thing if he had a full house. And if he somehow miraculously flopped two pair with nine-seven, the deuce on the turn is a terrible card for him because he's been coun-

"Should I call with king-high?"

terfeited – any overpair of mine beats him (aces, kings, queens). And that's my story: raised UTG and bet the flop. The whole thing seemed fishy to me – like he was trying to blow me off my hand...

I was pretty sure he didn't have a pair pre-flop or ace-high either – he would've gone all-in pre-flop (which he had been doing frequently). Why would he play a nine or seven this way? Wouldn't he go all-in on the flop with a pair that was vulnerable? (In case a face card peeled off on the turn like a king, jack, queen, or ace). The only hands that made sense to me were draws: ten-eight or eight-six for an open-ended straight draw. Maybe jack-ten for two overcards + a gutshot. Those hands made sense to me. Those hands had a plau-

---

10 You can always ask the dealer to count exactly how many chips someone has.

sible story. Those would play exactly this way: call pre-flop, call the flop, then try and bluff me on the turn – and king-high was beating all those hands.

"I think I have a better hand than you," I said and pushed my chips in to make the call. I turned over my king-jack-high – a bold statement. I couldn't have called praying to river a king or jack: my chances of winning against a nine were under 15 percent. My hand had to be the winner *as is*.

Pretty Boy grimaced and turned over 10♦-8♣ – the exact most likely hand I put him on. *Entirely consistent with his story.*

The river was inconsequential. He was eliminated and took 5th place prize money – a little more than $50 profit for more than five hours of play. We all chopped immediately after – myself the biggest stack taking "first" – and gleamed towards my father ("Dad, how'd I do?!").

Shout Out to the Guys

Nothing in poker has a 100% right answer. Even in the middle of a hand, you can make good, reasonable arguments for checking, calling, raising, and folding. Decisions, decisions. You're going to have more options than a 6'3" hunk who graduated from Harvard.

That's why it's important to weigh multiple perspectives. Thinking is its own art. Analyze accurately.

I wanted to give a shout out to some of my favorite Texas Hold'em hunks – and point you to them as a resource. One woman can't do it all!

YouTube is either a goldmine or landmine for poker commentary, depending whose channel you're watching. But there are a few expert poker coaches who really know their stuff. Jonathan Little posts a "Weekly Poker Hand" and livestream's his morning coffee so you can ask him all your pressing questions (Check or fold? Cream or sugar?) Bart Hanson hosts a weekly call-in show on his channel Crush Live Poker – a hidden gem for players of all levels. Anyone can call-in and receive personalized advice. He takes the $30 pots just as seriously as the $30,000 pots. The most famous YouTube commentator is high stakes pro Doug Polk, whose channel taught a writer girl like me to embrace math and numbers. And he wears tank tops. Super bro-like tank tops.

J. Little, Bart, and Doug are the ultimate one-man shows. That is, of course, if you find quips about 3-bet sizing entertaining.

Dr. Tricia Cardner from the "Poker Brain Science" chapter cohosts her "Poker on the Mind" podcast on iTunes.

YouTube shows and podcasts are free!

Jonathan Little

Teamwork!

One of the absolute best ways to get better at poker is by having poker friends. Discussing a hand with another person improves your own game tremendously. And hey, we always seem to know exactly what to do when we're giving advice to someone else.

The Poker Guys' YouTube channel and podcast features a rare duo, analyzing hands together as a team. *Awww...!*

I asked them to do an analysis on a real hand so you can have an example for what a breakdown looks like, modeling more advanced banter. This is hardcore technical pokerspeak. Bet you would've never guessed one of the lessons in this book was how to talk!

You learn a language by practicing speaking it with others.

David vs. Goliath!

This hand is Pro vs. Amateur. The pro poker player paid €5,300 to enter a tournament, and the amateur won a ticket for only $5! Since there are hundreds of thousands of dollars on the line and the amateur only has $5 invested, the pro makes some assumptions...

Check out this analysis from Jonathan and Grant (a.k.a. The Poker Guys). This is a hand from the PokerStars and Monte-Carlo EPT Main Event which took place April 28 - May 6, 2018. The buy-in was €5,300.

The Situation: 9 of 777 players remain in the EPT Monte Carlo Main Event. The current payout is 54k euro, first place is 712k. The blinds are 30k/60k.

The Action

Tomas Jozonis, a professional poker player, raises to 125k in late position with A♦-K♠. He has a stack of 3 million.

Kristin Gyorgi, an amateur who qualified for this event for about five bucks, re-raises from the small blind with 7♣-2♠ to 360k. He started the hand with 2.4m chips.

Jonathan: This is an ambitious re-raise, to say the least.

Grant: I really wouldn't expect this out of a guy who got in this thing for only five bucks, but here we are.

Jonathan: There's no obvious reason he's doing this... maybe this is how he made the final table? By losing his mind a lot?

Grant: Seems...bad.

> Tomas Jozonis calls.

Grant: Wow, didn't expect just a call. The positions and stacks seem correct for Tomas to put in a big raise in an attempt to get all in.

Jonathan: Maybe he thinks the amateur would never do this without a huge hand and he's just being very careful.

Grant: That's a typical way to profile a guy who has never been in a spot this big. I guess he just doesn't know much about Gyorgyi.

Jonathan: At the same point, A-K is such a good hand and it makes it less likely that Gyorgi has A-A or K-K. I think Tomas should be comfortable getting it in here to try to win a big pot and set himself up to potentially win the tournament. It's not a bad time to flip with all that money on top.

Grant: And, as we see, if Tomas were to put a big raise in he would just get to win the money in the middle without a sweat.

> The pot is now 840k. The flop comes Q♦-10♦-9♦, all diamonds.
>
> Gyorgyi (who still has 7♣-2♠ with no diamonds) bets 500k.
>
> Tomas Jozonis calls.

Grant: WHAT?!

Jonathan: This seems like an absolutely perfect spot for Tomas Jozonis to shove all in.

Grant: 100% agree. There is no hand that we fear with the nut flush draw and a gutshot straight draw. It would also be GREAT if our opponent just folded.

Jonathan: Yeah... and if we get called we might be able to win with an ace or king some of the time.

Grant: Well, we know he's up against 7♣-2♠, but Jozonis may be thinking that his opponent is tight enough that there aren't many hands he can have, having re-raised pre-flop, that would miss this flop and garner a fold.

Jonathan: But of course, we don't care. We don't mind if he calls. We're happy if he folds, slightly less happy if he calls, but either is *fine*.

> There is now 1.84m in the pot. Gyorgi has 1.52m left. The turn is is the 4♣.
>
> Gyorgyi *MOVES ALL IN*.
>
> Tomas Jozonis thinks for a while, and folds.

Grant: Well that hand was a complete trash fire.

Jonathan: This is one of the problems with just calling on the flop, and even pre-flop: you can get bluffed off a hand where you want to get to the river.

Grant: So why the heck did he fold?

Jonathan: If Gyorgyi has K-K, J-J, A-Q, or set, he's not getting the right price to call this bet with only one card to come. It just never should have come to this.

Grant: It seems Tomas' critical mistake was assuming Gyorgyi was far tighter than he actually is.

Jonathan: Seeing as Gyorgyi has 7♣-2♠, I feel compelled to agree with you.

> ### Talking Back
>
> **Amanda:** If a diamond/scare card rolled off on the turn, do you think Gyorgyi would have continued bluffing?
>
> **Grant:** Absolutely, this guy probably can't stop bluffing once he starts.
>
> **Jonathan:** You don't raise with 7-2 to give up when a scare card comes. You raise it to bet that scare card.

Final result?

The amateur turned his $5 investment into €184,000. The pro won €308,000.

♠♠ Quiz Level Three: Spades ♠♠

Keep track of your answers. Correct answers are worth 10 points!

1) What is "GTO"?

a) Gym, tan, laund[1] (hmm, I'm stumped).

b) Classical poker strategy.

c) Game Theory Optimal.

d) Game Time Omission.

2) Is it better to make the right decision 1x or 1,000x?

a) 1x.

b) 1,000x.

c) Depends if your strategy is GTO or Exploitative.

3) "Fold out better, get called by..."

a) The nuts.

b) The second-nuts.

c) Worse.

d) Sorry, no calls. Text only, please.

4) What is "table image?"

a) A reason to call someone's bluff.

b) How many loose or tight players are sitting at the same table.

c) A caption for a very boring thumbnail.

5) What's the best way for most people to get better at poker?

a) Bluff!

b) Call!

c) Bet!

d) Fold!

---

1 Jersey Shore.

6) True or False: Most people assume women raise a wide range of hands.

a) True.

b) False.

7) Finish the tournament poker saying: "The chips you lose are more important than the chips you..."

a) Gain.

b) Steal.

c) Re-buy.

8) True or False: You shouldn't bet small on the turn with a draw.

a) True.

b) False.

Answers on page 204.

Money Matters

I have two great fears in life: looking fat on-camera and going broke.

I have experienced both.

Poker is an expensive game, and my first few months included learning the hard way. I have also been tagged in many unflattering Facebook and Instagram photos.

There is an article I read when I first started playing poker, where a reporter interviews a friend who had just won three big tournaments[*]. He won these tourneys in a single month for a total profit of over $250,000. They go to dinner, and the tournament champ orders the cheapest dish on the menu. His drink? Tap water. When the reporter asks why, his friend says he still owes his poker investors $400,000 – and hasn't made a profit in over three years. He was living on loans.

At first, I thought this was an exaggeration. A fictionalized account. An article making a point. There is no way that a quarter-million dollars couldn't be a profit, let alone that other $400,000.

Now I find the story to be 100% believable.

Even players at the lowest stakes games carry around several Benjamins in their billfolds. To this day, I am amazed – and genuinely confused – by the amount of 20-somethings dropping thousands at casinos. They can't all be Bitcoin millionaires.

---

* Including the famed Sunday Million.

A GIRL'S GUIDE TO POKER

I like your big... bankroll

Money management is such a key concept in poker there's even a term for your investment resources: **bankroll**. This is your total poker fund.

A bankroll is how much money a person has solely for playing poker.

A professional poker player once told me his greatest edge is not the hours he spends studying (although those are many; he writes five-page essays about hands and keeps theme in a blue binder), the experience he has (he plays nearly every day), or the math skills he has (although he is a human calculator). He said his *real advantage comes from having a bigger bankroll* than the other players – something he learned from a fellow poker pro. Financial leeway allows him to make the most accurate decisions and cripple his competition.

PRO TIP

How handcuffed are you by your bankroll? Poker pros will happily risk $1,000 as a 55% favorite. Would you? If you are not comfortable committing your entire chip stack when you are a statistical favorite, you are probably playing too high stakes.

How large should your poker bankroll be?

The answer is more than you think.

You're not considered properly "rolled" for a cash game unless you have at least 20 buy-ins. Tournament bankroll standards are 100 buy-ins. It's not about how much money you have, it's how many buy-ins. Poker is an incredibly swingy game, and luck must always be accounted for if you want to play regularly. Literally!

> **The only way to cope with swings in poker is by having a proper bankroll.**

Whenever I wonder about bankroll, I always think about one hand from an episode of *Live at the Bike!*

Susie Q starts the hand with $8,450. Randall has $7,420. She has A♥-K♥. He has A♠-A♣. They get it all in pre-flop for what is just under a $15,000 pot. They decide to run it twice – which happens in high stakes games. The flop, turn, and river are dealt twice to mitigate dumb luck.

Randall is an 88% favorite to win the hand – *twice.*

The first time they run the deck, Susie Q wins with a flush. 4♦-10♥-5♠-9♥-J♥

The second time, Susie Q wins with a straight. Q♣-3♥-10♣-J♠-3♣

She wins both times and scoops the pot for $14,970.

The odds of this happening are 1.44%. That percentage is actually even lower because they ran it twice using the same deck meaning Susie Q can't use those same cards to make another flush.

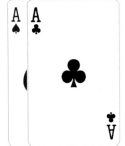

Randall *should* win 15 grand there nearly every time. No sports bet or stock option would ever give such good returns. (With those kinds of odds, you'd be foolish not to bet your house on it. Maybe even more.)

But he still lost, and 1.44% of the time you will lose too. Yikes.

Shot-taking

Shot-taking is when you play slightly above your means, hoping to hit big as a one-time trial.

There are mixed opinions on shot-taking. Some poker players swear by it – as in one big tournament catapulted their career. And especially if you are playing small stakes, one well-planned shot could transform your maneuverability. That said, it is a risk. Shot-take responsibly.

Staking... Poker Pros aren't as Rich as they Seem

When asking how many people a person has bedded, there used to be an old trick called the rule of three. Multiply a woman's answer

by three because most ladies want to seem choosy, and divide a man's answer by three because most men want to seem sexually experienced. The truth isn't nearly as impressive.

Same goes with poker. *Most poker players do not make nearly as much money as it seems.* Pros often don't keep the entirety of their profits; that's because they are *staked*.

It's hard to come up with, say, one million dollars (the entry fee for the bi-annual One Million for One Drop event), even if you're a top-level player. Instead poker pros often have their buy-ins (or substantial percentages of them) paid for by investors in return for a cut of profits – as if the investors are betting on a horse. And it's nothing to hee-haw about – poker staking, or "backing," is big business.

> Antonio Esfandiari won 18 million dollars in the 2012 One Drop tournament – and is estimated to have given around 16 million away to his backers. His take-home profit was even less after taxes.
>
> *Multi-million-dollar wins are extremely rare because most high stakes poker pros need to pay back their investors.*

How to Win $900,000 and Still Lose!

American poker pro and the internet's most famous strategy coach Doug Polk once shared in a YouTube video how he won $900,000 and still ended up in the red.

Doug lost around half a million dollars of his own money in 2014 against a player on-line. He rematched, this time staked with

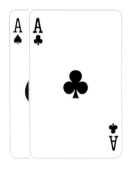

investors' money. The rematch earned him $900,000, but after paying back his investors plus factoring-in the cost of his earlier matchup, Doug walked away with a net loss. This included winning a massive A♠-A♣ versus K♥-K♠ cooler ($382,827, in case you were wondering).

Don't be fooled by big-dollar paydays. Poker comes with extremely high operating expenses! You've gotta spend money to make money.

"The first time I made a million dollars, I was 21-years-old. Six days later, I had $100,000," high stakes poker pro Bryn Kenney said in an interview. "The first time I had a big bankroll, I had 3.5 million. Five months later, I had negative $400,000."

Poker pro Gus Hansen's online losses total over $20 million – more than any online poker player has ever won. "Your on-line chronicles have been very well-documented in the high stakes world," Joey Ingram said to Gus on his podcast, "How do you feel looking back?" To which Gus replied, "There's always the quick three words: shoot me now."

Computers vs. Casinos

"The toughest game in the world is $0.25/$0.50 online," one professional poker player told me. "If you can beat that game, you can beat anything," he said while stacking up a rack full of chips. "At least $2/$5 in a casino."

Despite his backwards baseball cap and muscle tee, the young poker bro/pro made some excellent points. He told me he didn't go to college, but by the end of our conversation, I was certainly schooled.

Why Online Poker is Tougher

At first blush, saying it's harder to play for quarters online than hundreds in a casino seems silly. Why would *less money* make playing *more difficult?*

The truth is, it's not actually less money – for your opponents. Online opens you up to player pools all over the world – including places where $1.00 means much more than to the average American. *You* think you're playing $0.25/$0.50. *They* think they're playing $5/$10. For this reason, players will be more conservative.

The biggest shock for me when I started playing online was how much harder it is to get paid off.

In live casinos and home games, people call down with anything. They're curious. They're drinking. They're having fun. *They're trying to look like a hero* at the table picking off a big bluff – especially if the bluffer is a girl. For online players, it's just not

worth it (in more ways than one).

Dollars, euros, and pesos aside, online you're almost always against *younger players*. Teenagers don't have a lot of money. Doesn't matter where you are. And if for some reason a 23-year-old is making serious bank, they're probably not going to be messing around on their laptop gambling for quarters. The online stereotype is a hyper-studious nerdy little high school kid. Not some wannabe baller.

♦ Nearly every online poker player has software tracking their opponents' decisions.

♦ Be wary of poker-playing bots![1]

♦ "Rabbit hunting" is a fun feature online which allows you (if you've already folded) to see what the next card would've been.

---

1 Online poker robots.

Warp Speed!

Hurry, hurry, hurry! Put down your phone. Stop texting, stop looking at Facebook. Don't make a trip to the kitchen for another bag of chips. You don't have time.

Live poker is *leisurely*. Chat up the dealer, drink your cocktail, go for a walk. The pace is very slow. Most of the time you won't even be playing. Online, you're playing constantly. Live poker tables average 30 hands/hour, but online tables can easily average more than 100 hands/hour. You'll be exposed to more hands than trying to push through a crowded club.

Most online players *multi-table* – play numerous tables at once. Online games are also much more likely to be *short-handed*[2] meaning fewer than nine players. Most casino poker tables are nine-handed. Most online tables are six-handed. As a result, everyone will see many, many more flops, turns, and rivers. Pump up the volume.

PRO TIP

Fast, fast, fast! Live poker tables average 30 hands/hour, but online tables can easily average 100+. Multi-tabling can increase this total dramatically.

Kids playing online for six months may have more experience than adults playing for decades.

---

2 Short-handed play is much more aggressive since you're forced to play more frequently.

Desktop Jockey

Online microstakes can feel like pulling teeth sometimes. You're fighting tooth-and-nail for pennies. There are times playing online where winning $33 made me feel insanely rich. *MTV Cribs*, here I come.

When you're starting out, there's no reason to enter a $25 tournament – those add-up – but definitely consider several $2 and $3 tourneys. It's a good way to gather experience, and gameplay is a step up from the nickel and dime buy-ins. You'll start to play real poker!

Generally online poker is *not for gambling*. Most are there to study or win money. Few people want to "gamble" seventy-five cents – *except in tournaments*. You can find casual players in $5, $10, and $15 tournaments. The $0.55 tourneys are super sloppy and loose (remind you of any friends?) And don't get me started on the freerolls[3].

There are many amateur players in low stakes online tourneys.

Small stakes online events are easier than microstakes cash games.

Why Online Poker is Better

Online is not all doom and gloom. Affordable tourneys are a bright spot, and you can buy-in to poker games of all levels for reasonable amounts. Not as much to risk, but so, so much to gain.

---

3 Freerolls are tournaments you can enter for free but win real money.

Especially because you can play real poker.

Live casinos are filled with low stakes *luckfests* – games with very few big blinds and a huge rake.

They are extremely hard to beat over time.

Profiting at a casino $1/$2 game with a $100 max buy-in is a fool's gamble[4]. Skill doesn't really matter in those games; they're designed so everyone can win, and every dog has its day.

But online poker allows you to buy-in for 100 big blinds and *play proper poker*. Trying to build up a poker bankroll with $500 playing live is a suicide mission[5]. Doing so online is very possible. The poker dream lives!

Online poker rewards skill.

$500 or $10,000?

In late 2018, professional poker player and author Jonathan Little pitched a "gotcha" question on his social media accounts: "Would You Rather Begin Your Poker Career with $500 15 Years Ago or $10,000 Today?" Most non-poker people (do those exist?) would take the 10 grand. Duh.

His followers said the obvious right answer is $500 15 years ago back when poker was easier. No brainer. So which is it?

Jonathan, the diplomat that he is, explained the merits of both. Some players may fare better with a $10,000 boost today – especially if they use the money to purchase training tools and coaching (teacher's pets! Rich teacher's pets.) But he admitted if it were him needing to start over, he, too, would rather take the $500[6]. Poker was just that different.

---

4 "Fool's gamble." Get it?

5 Trust me, I've tried!

6 Every successful poker player I asked chose $500 15 years ago without hesitation, including commentator and coach Bart Hanson.

Dad Knows Best

My dad has been playing cash games for years, and is what most would consider a "good reg"[7] at the $5/$10 level.

But until his daughter started writing a poker book, *he had never entered a tournament*. And once he did, he didn't do so well – cash game strategy is way different from tourney strategy. He was getting crushed. So he started playing freerolls – tournaments you enter for free and win real money – to practice playing tourneys.

Mind you, freerolls are not exactly what one would call "fun". They are a unique form of torture. My dad would play average ones with between 250 and 750 players that last around seven hours. Only the top 10 would get paid; the rest win nothing. Tenth won $0.55. First place won $2.50. Talk about tedious. Painfully, painfully tedious.

On top of this, my father's go-to game is $5/$10 – the buy-in is usually $500 *minimum*. People buy-in for thousands. But I was getting texts from my mother saying that my dad had stayed up until 4:00am fervently trying to win two dollars.

But you know what? It worked.

Pretty soon I was getting "final table" texts from my dad's daily freeroll. He started to figure it out[8]. He started to do well. And before I knew it, his online bankroll swelled to a whopping $4.50. Money entirely made in freerolls.

More importantly, my dad now knew what he was doing wrong playing live tournaments like a cash game. *He learned tournament strategy*. And he learned online tourney strategy – which is 10x more aggressive.

---

7 Good regular player. Opposite is "bad reg" – someone who plays all the time but loses.
8 My dad says the key is surviving the insane gamble craziness at the beginning, and then the real poker begins.

Let me Hear Your Body Talk

The first printed book was written in German. The second-most commonly spoken language in the world is Spanish. NASA requires all its astronauts to learn Russian.

But there ain't no language like body language.

Old school poker glamorized getting a "read" on someone. A scratch on the nose, a flick of the wrist, a glimmer in the eye – little giveaways whether they were bluffing or had you beat. Flirtatious wisdom that made poker seem like Hollywood romance.

Call me crazy/twenty-five[1], but I've never been exceptionally good at tells. Don't get me wrong, I'll get a read here or there – one time I almost insanely folded a full house because the guy's demeanor seemed so strong; sure enough, he had quads – but it's hard for me to find a clear tick. Kids with computers these days! I'm more comfortable assessing someone's emojis than emotions[2].

The Three Big Tells

That said, there are a few *tried-and-true tells* that even a clueless millennial like me can pick up on. Here are the top three.

1) Strong Means Weak

When someone has a very big hand, they will often shrink into a meek little mouse, looking downtrodden, disappointed, and just plain sad. Don't fall for it. This is the oldest trick in the book – *if someone was bluffing, would they want you to think they're weak?* No! People puff up their chest and act aggressively when they're trying to scare you – not encourage a call. Tough guys ain't so tough – it's the quiet ones that'll get ya.

---

1 But I will be 26 once this book is published. Buy an extra copy for my birthday.
2 Back when I was on the dating app scene where you start talking to someone through text, I had a homefield advantage: I was a writer. This became a problem because it was way easier to make a guy fall in love with me over words than wine. Whoops!

170

2) Lightning Speed

Quick actions means quick decisions. When someone *snapcalls* – calls a bet instantly – they almost always have a medium-strength hand like a single pair or flush draw. Why is this? Because if they had a strong hand like two-pair, a set, or combo draw, they'd contemplate raising. And when someone flops a weird double-gutter[3] or something like that, they need to study the board so they're not confused. But holding J♥-10♥

> **PRO TIP**
> **"How much?"**
> When someone asks in a soft baby voice "how much?" a bet size is, run. They're usually crazy strong.

---

3 Funky gutshot straight draws on both ends. Such as holding J-10 when the flop is K-9-7 (either a queen or eight will make you a straight). Or 8-6 on 10-7-4 where you need a nine or five.

on the flop A♣-10♠-3♥? Almost always a crystal clear just call spot and see what happens. Not much to think about. But J♥-10♥ on A♣-10♠-10♣? Now we're wondering. Hmm. People also call draws fast. If someone has J♦-9♦ on K♣-8♦-2♦, they know they're not folding and are unlikely to raise, so will probably insta-call. They do for two reasons:

1) They have an easy decision.

2) They don't want to be blown off their hand – facing a monster bet on a non-diamond turn is not what they want to see.

So they act fast to pressure you against betting big. It's an intimidation tactic to get cheap cards.

3) Posturing
When you're considering betting, players will preemptively handle their chips – they're trying to let you know they're going to call so you don't bet too big. But if someone had a really good hand, they wouldn't do this. They wouldn't be trying to scare you.

Freeze, Woman!

Uh-oh. Caught bluffing? Don't choke up! Generally players with good hands are confident, comfortable, and ready to talk. Chatty Cathy wants a call[4].

Bluffers prefer to keep quiet.

They don't want to give anything away. What if they crack?

Rapid eye movements indicate *curiosity, excitement, and interest*. When bluffing, even the eyes freeze up! "They're going to call – I can't look!"

---

4 Clearly.

Double Bubble Bluff

One of my absolute favorite poker plays was thwarted by body language.

We were a few hours into a tournament, and I defended my big blind with J♣-8♣. The flop was 10♣-10♠-3♣. I checked, he bet, I called. Turn: 9♦. I opted for a check, he bet, and once again I decided to call. The river was a blank (didn't matter). I checked again, he bet – *I went all-in.*

Checkraised the river all-in for his entire stack. Mega bluff.

He kept shaking his head, extremely distressed. "I knew I should've checked!"

He kept glancing over at me, trying to get a read.

Then, finally, he made the call (two kings).

"You have a tell," he told me on the break. "You were chewing gum, and stopped chewing. Froze up. That's the only reason I called." So long, spearmint!

Don't Try to Change Me

Tips and tricks aside, there is one ultimate end-all, be-all thing to look for: *change* (*changing the course of action* in pokerspeak). When someone doesn't like the way a situation is going, they try and switch gears. Said another way, when someone likes what's happening, they do everything in their power to keep things exactly as they are. Let's say you go all-in with an awesome hand, and your opponent has picked up their chips, nanoseconds away from calling you. No way on earth you'd shout, "Stop!" No way you'd say anything at all. Don't break the flow when it's going in your favor.

A perfect demonstration of this[5] is on an older high stakes poker tournament, where pro Phil Laak goes all-in as a bluff in a fun, sloppy manner. The other player, Brian Rast, stands up and agonizes – on the brink of calling. Brian talks about how cool his call with ace-high would be on TV, and how he won't respect himself if he folds. "There's more important things than money in life," he says, "I kinda wanna do it." At this moment, Phil turns around and *opens a water bottle*. The instant Brian folds, poker pro Antonio Esfandiari – who went on to be winner of the biggest tournament payout in poker history for $18,346,673 – chides that's the oldest tell in the book! "You gave it away at the end. One-hundred percent," he tells Phil.

"What'd I say?" Phil replies.

Antonio tells him he moved to take a sip of water. "If you want him to call, you wouldn't do anything to change course of action."

Hero Call

My own personal best hero-call was in a hand I played terribly, but made an excellent point about body language.

I was at the MGM National Harbor playing their $1/$3 (buy-in is for $100-$500) game and had a little over $600 in front of me – a lot for a 24-year-old writer girl working at a non-profit. This was my last buy-in too. If I lost it, I was leaving. Couldn't call bets for funsies.

I raised to $20-ish ($22 I believe) with A♠-Q♣ and was reraised to $75. Most of the time I'd just fold here – players at these stakes generally only reraise with very, very good hands. My ace-queen is usually going to be crushed.

But I had played this guy once before, and remembered he liked to pull moves. I actually thought my ace-queen may've been ahead. Against this player – and against this player only – my feeling was I had the best hand. I called.

---

5 Watch the clip on my website amandasaces.com in the BodyTalk quiz.

Flop: 7♠-7♣-5♦. Boring. Dry as the Sahara. I checked, he checked.

Turn: 10♥. I bet $75 (not sure exactly my reasoning). He smooth-called.

River: K♠. I bet $175, and he went all-in for about $300 more. FML.

A big leak in my game was making decisions too quickly, but this time something felt off – I actually asked the dealer for a count[6]. If I called and was wrong, I'd only have $60 left. But if I folded now, I'd still have about $300 in front of me – plenty of room to play.

Then there was the problem I didn't have anything but ace-high.

In my mind, the king on the river was a good card for me – now it was less likely he had ace-king because there was a king on the board. But more importantly, I thought the whole hand through from start-to-finish. I wasn't calling $75 pre-flop with ace-queen praying to hit a queen – unlikely to happen. I only called because I thought my hand was good – *as is*.

---

6 Asking for a count means having the dealer tell you the *exact* bet amount.

Nothing on that board would've changed that assumption. I was already losing to ace-king, so the king on the river was a non-factor to me, and if anything, made my hand better. His value hands were pocket pairs I was already losing to; it was doubtful he reraised me pre-flop with some sort of seven.

"What do you have?" he finally asked me.

"Ace-high," I said. "Ace-queen."

"I don't believe you!" he replied earnestly. "Show me."

I flashed him my ace-queen. "But I think I'm going to call you," I said putting my chips over the line to make the call.

"I'll show you one!" he exclaimed (my chips were literally hovering over the line mid-air – once I drop them, it's a call).

I pointed to his right-hand card. He flipped it over: ace. I called instantly[7].

"Good call," he muttered and tossed his hand in the muck. Must've had a worse ace.

At the time, I wasn't sophisticated enough to know "changing the course of action" tells. And to be honest, I didn't have any gut instinct or body language or intuition reads on him – he didn't give anything away – I was making a game theory decision. GTO emphasizes *distribution* – how many times do my cards beat player X's cards – whereas exploitative strategy focuses on reading people.

---

7 I hadn't thought through which cards would make me call or fold exactly. A king or ten I obviously fold since those cards are on the board. A queen would give me pause. But I'd pretty much made up my mind, and the ace made his value range a lot slimmer: pocket aces or nothing.

My thinking was if my cards were good pre-flop, they were good on that runout too.

When I spoke with more seasoned poker players, they said once he tries to show me a card, it's an instacall. My chips were in mid-air a split-second away from calling, and he was trying to change my mind. No way he does that with kings full or quad tens.

Ask the Expert: This is a Case for the F.B.I.!

In researching this book, I consulted with someone who knows far more than me about body language secrets: Former F.B.I. special agent Joe Navarro. He is the author of several best-selling books, including *What Every BODY Is Saying: An Ex-FBI Agent's Guide to Speed-Reading People* and *Phil Hellmuth Presents Read 'Em and Reap: A Career FBI Agent's Guide to Decoding Poker Tells*[8].

---

8 Phil Hellmuth – one of the most famous players of all-time – authored his autobiography with my same publisher: D&B Poker. Check out *Poker Brat* on dandbpoker.com.

I started by asking him the burning question: *sunglasses*. What did he think about shades at the table? Joe was non-partial – *it depends how much you give away with your eyes*. Some people give away more with their posture. Others their smile. Others their feet (this is a big one, he says).

Sunglasses are fine for confidence, but his main concern was using them as a crutch. When the shades are on, people don't think they need to monitor the rest of their body language. And according to Joe, *everything* matters.

It's not all about having a good poker face. It's also about having a good poker body. Jittery feet, slumped shoulders, and backwards leans are major giveaways. *Your posture is a super tell.* No one wants to be described as "a bad body but with a pretty face" – don't be the poker face equivalent!

Sunglasses boost confidence because people can't see where you're looking.

The New Normal

The key to poker body language is a *baseline* – what's your neutral? Wait a few seconds before making a decision so you don't switch from lightening quick decisions to all of a sudden tanking (thinking long and hard). Keep your hands in the same place (pros like rested on the shoulder). Shuffle your chips at the same constant speed. *A tell is really just something someone does away from their norm* – perking up in their chair, reaching for chips sloppily, going quiet – so establish a nice neutral baseline.

A tell is...

Welcome to Vegas!

Congratulations! – you're through with the poker how-to guide. No more strategy or explanations[1]. Mazel tov, girl. Time to celebrate! *Let's get you to Vegas.*

A little last-minute advice before you outgrow me: Not all casinos are alike. Not all cardrooms have the same buy-ins, players, or ambience. (Although if your ambition is to be a poker pro, your biggest concerns should be rake, rake, and rake!).

When you travel to Vegas to play poker for the first time, where should you go?

Different cardrooms are better for different things – it all depends what you're looking for. As a *Girl's Guide* research project, I went to all the cardrooms on the Las Vegas strip to provide recommendations[2] and will share with you my favorites in each category.

Vegas Reviews

Poker rooms visited: MGM, Caesars, Mirage, Flamingo, Harrah's, Bally's, Treasure Island, Bellagio, Wynn, Aria, Mandalay Bay, Excalibur, Bellagio, Venetian, Planet Hollywood[3].

Most entry-level games were $1/$2 or $1/$3 with ($100-$200 or $100-$300 buy-in unless stated otherwise.)

Best for Beginners

My vote is for The Mirage. Never heard of it? Neither have the pros – it's very amateurish and beginner-friendly. I picked it because it's calm and nicely balances real play without being too intimidating. The poker area is *cute, clean, and pink* – an old Hollywood vibe with

---

1 Sequel, anyone?
2 I did this during July 2018.
3 I visited during the World Series of Poker which changed the set-up at the Rio.

a slot machine display from a different era. There weren't many wild gamblers which makes the game more approachable. I found it *easy to focus* and *not stressful*.

Great for truly playing poker without distraction.

Slot machines in the background aren't as loud, and there isn't as much runoff from the Vegas party scene. A hidden find – literally. It's hard to find. That's a good thing.

Sleeper Hit

The biggest surprise by far was Mandalay Bay – it's beautiful! Lovely poker room with gorgeous ocean blue felt and elegant wood triangles carved into the ceiling. The lighting was nice too – poker rooms vary between eyestrain darkness or overly bright and tacky. Mandalay Bay was easy to see in. Even the air had a soft perfume! Most of the players were older men. I didn't see any young guys, girls, or drunks. Closest thing to playing poker at a fancy country club.

The cardroom for men who play golf.

Real Poker Starts Here

When it comes to playing a good game, it's hard to top the Wynn. This is where I spent the most time playing outside of research purposes. The poker room is *contemporary, clean, and professionally designed in art deco* – there are giant paintings of playing cards in primary colors. Red, yellow, blue, and cubist. There are many tables – one of the most expansive poker rooms in Vegas – with wealthy players.

> ## Better Buy-ins
> **The Wynn, Harrah's and sometimes Treasure Island all have a $1/$3 with a $100-$500 max.**

Finances in mind, this is a place where good players can make money.

Especially because the Wynn has a well-structured game. Their $1/$3 is a $100-$500 buy-in – meaning you can play deep-stacked. Remember from the very beginning chapter of this book that the fewer blinds there are relative to the buy-in, the more the game becomes a luckfest. The Wynn's structure rewards skilled players.

Bring Your Friends

Caesars Palace is good when visiting Vegas with non-poker play-ing friends or you're not sure if you want to spend the whole night playing cards too seriously. It's *extremely central* – inside and out. Caesars is on the strip, *close to everything*; you can easily casi-no-hop. And their small little dome poker room seems like it was plopped-in randomly with the mix. The poker room is cramped and lackluster – plus I found myself making mistakes with the slidey hard-to-hold chips – but it's got *location, location, location*. Into sports? You're practically part of the sports-betting area – possi-

bly within talk-to-your-friends distance – and look into *tons* of TV screens with a big bar. Everyone at the table got a round of shots. There's also a sexy restaurant five steps away with fiery lava lamps for décor.

Caesars is catch-all, be all. Great for poker one minute, restaurant dining another minute, taking shots the next minute.

Fear commitment?[4] Try Caesars.

Best Bang for Your Buck

Saying the Excalibur has a poker room is a bit of a stretch – it's more like a black cave that goes ding! ding! ding! Surrounded by slot machines, the Excalibur poker zone is very, very loud. And dark. And tiny. There are barely any tables. But it's the only poker game in Vegas with a *$60 buy-in* ($1/$2 with a $60-$300 cap). Their daily tournament is also only $40 and doesn't take so long because there are only a few players; it's closer to a mini-poker tournament called a sit'n'go. It's not a place for any serious poker player, but it's a good place to start if you just want to get a feel for the game. The play-

---

4 Ironically where I met my boyfriend. See next chapter.

ers are unintimidating – no sharks here! – and both the people and staff were exceptionally friendly.

No one plays at the Excalibur to be hardcore. They play to have fun.

Author's Choice

Another favorite of mine was the Aria[5]. There's not much bad to say about it – the chips are nice, the food is nice[6], the whole place is nice. Vegas provides free drinks – but the Aria has the only red wine which is *fantastic!* Better than most red wines I've paid for. Try the wine. Best dealers in Vegas too – professional and personable. As a woman playing poker, it's incredibly common for dealers to assume you're not going to raise, and rather just call, fold, or check. The Aria dealers were patient and present. I spent many, many hours playing there and liked them all. *Luxury experience.*

Unsurprisingly, the Aria is a favorite of people who already play poker.

My tables were full of European pros (good-looking!) and players with a good grasp of the game. You don't hear the slot machines, and it's not a drop-by kind of poker scene – *people are there to play*. Looking for happy-go-lucky guys who want to take tequila shots? Aria is not the place. But want an in-depth conversation about good turn cards to double-barrel? Take a seat. I spent hours enjoying the company of many fellow students of the game, and eventually was unsurprised to hear the Euro teen next to me asking my thoughts on an episode of Joey Ingram's podcast.

Bon Appétit!

My award for best food goes to the Venetian.

---

5 The Aria has the best rake structure for higher stakes.
6 The Aria has a lovely healthy restaurant/cafe next to the poker room open 24 hours.

Jersey Shore

Looking for hunk moves and junk foods? *Planet Holly-wood is practically a club.* First, there's nowhere good to sit – the chairs are super low (good luck seeing!) and un-comfortable. Then there are stripper girls dancing in bras and just more than a thong, with waitresses in fishnets. Hunk alert: all the hot, young guys go there too. Muscle tanks and bro hats. Just don't plan on talking to them – it's way too loud. *Most players are inexperienced.* This can lead to lots of tough-to-beat vari-ance – gambling and trying to get lucky. You may be thinking,

"great! Easy money!" Not necessarily. PH is big on the hit and run – a young guy will get lucky one hand and leave. People routinely buy-in short – for smaller amounts – which means it's tough to win a big pot. PH doesn't have a wealthy player pool; there are a lot of 21-year-old dudes gambling $150. More *Bingo!* than poker.

It's welcoming if you don't know how to play – most guys there don't know either. You won't feel pressured to play perfectly.

It's OK to make mistakes here. I spent nearly a week staying in a room at PH and wasn't a fan from a poker-perspective (or girl per-spective – hot chicks in bikinis weren't good for my self-esteem!), but it is very beginner-friendly. Guys openly didn't know how to play, and that was okay.

Your Guide to Dating Poker Players

When my friends asked me my thoughts on dating poker players, my answer was simple, "Don't!" I found my current boyfriend at a poker table in Vegas two days later.

I'm no dating expert – but I have been on a lot of dates. One of my first major articles ran on the weekend back cover of the *Los Angeles Times* about my experience using dating apps. During that time I probably met nearly every eligible bachelor in Los Angeles. *The Washington Post* also played matchmaker for me in its playful "Date Lab." Carrie Bradshaw, eat your heart out.

Yet all my time spent "researching" men didn't come close to the lessons I learned at the poker table.

Ever heard the expression "...if you were the last man/woman on Earth?" That's what it's like playing at a poker table.

The Good, the Bad, and the Ugly

Poker love is its own game; there are many variables.

Pros

Spend enough time on the felt, and you'll experience all sorts of emotions you never thought possible – win, lose, or chop. I can't tell

you how valuable it is having someone who can understand the pain of aces cracked. Or top set losing. Or busting on the bubble. Then there's the extreme elation when your flush draw comes in on the river in a big multiway pot. Not to mention someone who even knows what any of that

means. Hold'em is its own language, and there's nothing sexier than hearing, "that's a nice-looking turn... card." You're going to want someone who understands the poker psyche.

Ain't no date like a casino date!

Cons

Poker hours are crazy hours. The hardest thing about dating professional poker players is that it's dating someone with a night job. Primetime is on weekends. Be prepared for a sexy Wednesday afternoon lunch.

On a more candid level in dating poker guys, it often felt like I was competing with the casino. Poker is fun. So is making money. Why go see a movie when you can play cards? Seat open[1]. The real reason why I was gun-shy about dating poker players was my previous experience of constantly being put second[2]. Normal guys are hunkering for something to do on a Saturday night. Poker guys always have plans.

---

1 Poker slang for trying to get someone to sit down at the table.
2 This goes both ways: I have chosen poker over spending time with guys I truly liked.

Love Story

When my boyfriend and I first met at a poker table, we spent a few hours talking and flirting, and when I stood up to leave, he asked me out to dinner. I brushed him off saying, "No, you're a poker player, I won't keep you from the game. Do your thing!" To which he responded, *"There are more important things in life than poker."*

No poker guy had ever said that to me – my experience going out with cardplayers was always poker over date night. I hated feeling like I was holding them back and less fun.

We left for a restaurant right then and there.

I liked him, but was still skeptical if a poker guy could really make time. I played it coy, flaky on answering his text messages, a non-believer. But when we ran into each other at a poker table in Vegas two weeks later, I realized he wasn't bluffing[3]. I didn't win that night but couldn't have been any luckier.

Many guys and girls seek relationships because they are bored and want late-night company. Poker players never have that problem.

When I was tired by the whole dating app culture and bar scene, I fully preferred cardrooms to clubs.

Pro? Con? Both?

When you play poker with someone, you get to know them on a different level – *FAST*! How they handle wins. Losses. Alcohol. Junk food. Weirdos. Cocktail waitresses. No sleep. Stress.

---

3 He was the first person to purchase this book!

And you'll instantly be confronted with what's in a guy's pants **(corner pocket)**: his wallet. Live poker will quickly let you know how a guy feels about $500. And he'll also see *your* relationship with money.

When you meet someone for the first time in the "real world," it's usually for an hour or two. Maybe three if you are really hitting it off. Anything longer than that gets tiring, and almost always involves a change of location to a park, movie, or apartment (even I can't talk for five hours straight!). We mostly only see snapshots of each other on our best behavior.

Sit at the same poker table as someone and you'll easily spend 12 hours together. You're already on Date #3.

You're not going to always be in your most flattering light, and some things are better left to the imagination. It's hard *not* to be ugly at four in the morning. Gross hair, sweaty clothes, and short fuses.

By the same logic, it cuts the pretense. No more "OMG, wow, we both like vanilla!" smalltalk forever (or "what TV shows do you watch?" "What do you do for fun?" Cringe!) *You can learn more about a person when they are silent than when they are talking.* How does it feel to be in their space? Do you enjoy their company? *Are you comfortable?* Sit together long enough at a poker table and you'll get answers to the right questions.

Meeting men at a poker table is about their energy. Not their resumé.

Husband Hunting

Before entering the poker world, I viewed dating like a marketing pitch – here's who I am and what I have to offer. This is my job, my hair, my apartment. Sign on the dotted line, please.

When I went on dates, I "interviewed" men – and expected them to interview me. A match meant satisfying each other's checklists. That didn't go so well. *Even if we were compatible on paper, we didn't click in our daily lives.* It was all artificial.

Playing poker was an escape from the dating game, and ironically caused me to spend more time with men in six months than I had in six years. And I learned more than any dating book, workshop, or even happily-coupled-up friend could have ever told me.

Namely how to chill out. Stopping with all the "getting to know you" questions; getting to know someone can have more to do with the way they order an Irish Mule than where they went to college. Their mannerisms. Their attitude. Their focus. How they handle a loss. A win. Tabletalk. Humor. Feeling glee or remorse after beating someone out of a major pot. Sympathy. *I started relating to men as people rather than prototypes.* They were my friends.

You can't be "on" all the time when playing poker binges. Eventually you need to let your hair down and relax.

The author and boyfriend one year after meeting at a poker table.

World's Best Dating Advice

One time I met a guy while playing cards – we were chatty, casual, and had chemistry. I thought he looked like a movie star in a leather jacket but didn't lose my cool. Guys were a dime-a-dozen in the poker world – no need to go gaga for Gosling.

A few hours later I picked up my chips, and he made sure to get my contact info. I didn't agree to dinner, but I said next time he was playing, I'd join. We entered a tournament together that week and hung out until I finally agreed to meet for dinner away from the casino.

Our first date was awful. A total disaster.

A week later, we talked about it as friends. He said it was like going out with a different person. As though I was reading from a "script." I had snapped into date-mode autopilot. Canned and cringy.

As cheesy as it sounds, he told me I should've just been myself.

I finally understood what that meant.

Casino Cheat Sheet

Never been to a casino before? Or maybe you've been to a casino – but still feel clueless? Never fear: your **Casino Cheat Sheet** is here!

Before You Go

You will need:

- ◆ **Wallet with ID card.** Most casinos check ID. Credit cards are NOT accepted

- ◆ **Large bills.** Poker tables don't take any bills smaller than $20s, and casino ATMS have high fees. They're also strict with buy-ins: you cannot sit down or rebuy at a $200 table with $195.

- ◆ **Phone charging cord.** Many poker tables have USB ports for each seat – you'll never know how long you end up staying!

- ♦ **Jacket.** Don't freeze!

- ♦ **Gum, Mints.** Not necessarily for you! If you have the bad luck of sitting next to someone with tuna sandwich or all-nighter breath, you're going to want to get out your mints, and "casually" ask if anyone else would like one as well.

Free apps such as Poker Atlas and Bravo Poker will tell you how many poker tables are available, wait lists, and buy-in costs.

Look up poker tournaments on a casino's website or app.

Use a rideshare app or valet! You don't want to be walking to your car alone at night with wads of poker cash. This goes for guys and girls.

When You Arrive

First thing you're going to want to do is ask where to get a "player's card" and get one printed. This allows you to get comps, receive prizes, and enter tournaments. Also free food!

The casino will have a designated *poker room*, which is not always a room. More like a "poker area."

At the front of the poker room, there will be a screen with a list of games.

The screens are condensed and confusing – prepare to decode! "$1/$3; $100-$500" is a game where you can buy-in for anywhere between $100 and $500. The blinds will be $1/$3. Underneath the numbers, you'll see a list of letters: "AB, SC, ZZ" or "JAX" and "~AB." These are people's initials on the waitlist. Casinos will sometimes add "~" to signify a female player.

> **Here's what you say:**
>
> "Can you put [YOUR INITIALS] on the list for the $1/$3? game"
>
> **Or, if you want to sound really cool, just say:**
>
> "Can you put [YOUR INITIALS] on the $1/$3?"

Don't be afraid to ask questions before choosing a game too.

Chips, Please!

Many casinos let you buy chips at the table. As soon as you sit down, an employee will come up behind you and ask, "what are you buying-in for?" or "how much do you need?" These people are *chiprunners*. You hand them your cash, and they return with your chips. Otherwise you need to purchase chips from the poker sign-up area (where the wait lists are) or from the *cashier cage*.

Buying chips at the table can make even the most confident players feel self-conscious. Everyone will be watching you intently, including eyeing the bill denominations in your wallet. The chiprunner will also expect you to know how many chips you want right away.

You can always purchase chips in advance at the cashier's cage instead and bring them to the table – which everyone will appreciate! It frees up the staff and speeds up the game.

Open Seat!

If there is more than one seat available, try and sit to the left of an-yone with a large chipstack or looks a little gambly. Sitting to their left will allow you to see what they do first so you aren't surprised by a "Big Stack Bully."

Never feel like you have to stay at any seat! You can always move – either to a different seat at the same table or a new table entirely.

When you sit down, the dealer will ask if you want to "play now" or "wait". Playing now will require paying a small fee, or you can enter for free if you wait a few turns. Waiting also provides the advantage of familiarizing yourself with other players and pace of the game. Ask the dealer if you need help, but it's usually just best to wait.

Stack Strategy

 ♦ Organize your chips into stacks of 20 or taller. Anything less looks weird.

 ♦ Keep high-denomination chips easily visible. Do NOT play hide-and-seek with $100+ chips – if other players cannot see your high-value chips, you will get in trouble.

 ♦ Don't mix colors! This is called a *dirty stack*.

Can You Talk?

You can talk to the players next to you about anything you want – *except* the current hand. Do not say, "Someone's got a flush!" or "She's totally bluffing!" Anything that changes a person's decision – "influences the action" – is majorly forbidden. You can't give someone advice while they're thinking. *If you're playing the hand,*

you're allowed to talk cards only if it's just between you and another player (e.g. "Why'd you bet so much? Are you trying to get me to fold?") You can talk TV shows and Mai Tais all you want but keep the strategizing zipped.

After the hand is over, you're allowed to say anything you want, including card commentary. ESPN Poker, here you come.

Gameplay Rules

♦ Wait your turn! Don't fold before it's your chance to act.

♦ When you call someone's bet on the river, you're paying to see their hand, even if they tell you what they have.

♦ Always ask the dealer, "Who has to show first?" Avoid revealing your cards at all costs.

♦ Tossing in a single chip counts as a call. If someone goes all-in for $1,000 and you toss even a single chip over the line, you're calling their bet. Same goes for raises. Let's say you want to raise to $25. Doesn't matter if you throw-in a $25 chip, $50 chip, or $100 chip – a single chip is just a call.

♦ Phones are allowed after hands, but not during.

♦ You can't take chips off the table and put them in your purse or pocket.

♦ If you don't want to risk all your winnings, ask for a table change and buy-in again for less. Not all casinos allow this.

♦ If you have any problems, ask to call the floor (short for floorman). It's their job to referee foul play. Anything from chip confusions to dealer mistakes to temper tantrums.

♦ Tip the dealer after any pots you win.

♦ The bigger the pot, the bigger the expected tip. One dollar after winning a $30 pot is perfectly reasonable, but $1 after winning $300 looks stingy.

♦ You can leave a poker table whenever you want for 20-30 minutes at a time.

The #1 Most Important Rule!

Verbal is binding!

You are 100% committed to what you say. Joking around, "I'm all-in" is not funny – you will have to go all-in then. Saying "raise," "call," or "fold" is just as final as physically doing so.

Trouble counting chips?

Announce your bet. Say, "Bet $25" or simply, "$25" which prevents any counting mistakes and helps the game go faster.

Jargon, Jargon, Jargon!

Wanna learn some slang?

Hop on the felt.

Poker tables are so loaded with lingo you may not think the game's in English. You'll hear everything from "wash the cards" to "don't splash the pot," to "he hit the gutter" – and those are just terms that have to do with water! Don't fret when someone says a board is exceptionally "wet." You'll be talking "coolers" and "heaters" soon enough[1].

1 Try the Pokerspeak jargon quiz or the Casino Trip adventure on amandsaces.com.

◆◆ Quiz Level Four: Diamonds ◆◆

Keep track of your answers. Correct answers are worth 10 points!

1) What is a bankroll?

a) If you have to ask, you can't afford it.

b) The amount of money you have set aside to play poker.

c) A really bland kind of pastry.

d) When you spend your entire paycheck on sashimi.

2) The average poker player will see more hands in six weeks on a computer than six months in a casino.

a) Kids these days…

b) Six months? More like six years.

c) I'm not a nerd.

d) Yes, but you forgot to multiply the number of hands in a casino by number of drinks.

3) Bring breath mints at a casino for…

a) Yourself.

b) The hot guy sitting two seats over.

c) Who needs breath mints after eating a casino hamburger at 6 o' clock in the morning?

d) The players, the dealer, the entire casino staff… Everyone. Please.

e) Is this a quiz question or Public Service Announcement?

4) Body language secrets are…

a) Ooh… sounds sexy!

b) Why some girls get all the guys.

c) Rapid eye movement, shrinking posture, and changes in the course of action.

d) More observable in someone's eyes than mouth.

5) True or False: The most important factor in analyzing someone's body language is knowing their normal.

a) True. Verified by F.B.I. secret agents.

b) False. It's a myth that people have a body language baseline.

6) Match the Vegas casino (a-d) with the description (1-4)

a) Mandalay Bay.

b) Wynn.

c) Aria.

d) Planet Hollywood.

1) Pretty with bright blue tables. Where the Little Mermaid would play poker if Atlantica smelled like perfume.

2) Party bros and go-go girls.

3) Good food and good players.

4) A choice for people with *lots* of money. And perhaps you too will make lots of money here because they have some of the best game structures - then spend it all two steps away buying a designer purse.

7) True or False: Poker shows you different sides of a person.

a) True.

b) False.

c) I've already seen too much!

8) To win at poker and at life, you must...

a) Be results-oriented.

b) Achieve a positive return ROI[1].

c) Buy copies of *A Girl's Guide to Poker* to give to your friends.

d) Be yourself.

Answers on page 205.

---

1 Return on investment.

Quiz Answers

Quiz Level One: Clubs

Calculate your score. Ten points for each correct answer.

1) b, 2) b, 3) c, 4) d (1,471 hands), 5) d, 6) a, 7) b, 8) d

Word search: Storyteller, Bracelet, Poker, Emotions, Doyle, Pandora, Bluff, Think.

In poker, a very good player is called a shark, and a very bad player is called a fish!

0–30 points: Smells like fish

You're ready to play poker? Stop bluffing! Get back in the water.

40–60 points: Dolphin

Hey there, Flipper! Keep that tail moving – you're already doing well navigating the poker waters.

60–80 points: Ladyshark

Little fish better watch out when you're in the water! Go find Nemo.

> ### Fish out of Water
>
> **There's a common poker saying: "If you look around the table and don't know who the fish is, it's you!"**

Quiz Level Two: Hearts

Calculate your score. Ten points for each correct answer.

1) Blinds, rake, competition, 2) b, 3) a, 4) b, 5) a, 6) b, 7) d, 8) a, 9) a, 10) b, 11) a

Find which hand category you fall into based on your results.

0-40 points: Offsuit Three-gapper (6♦-2♣)

This doesn't look pretty now, does it? You and your cards aren't connected. Straighten-up your game if you want to be hitting straights.

50-80 points: Suited Broadways (K♥-Q♥)

Now this is a girl with possibilities! You've still got room for "improvement," but keep working and you'll be on-stage in no time.

90-110 points: Pocket Rockets (A♦-A♣)

Congratulations – you "aced" it! It must feel lonely being at the top... of your range.

Quiz Level Three: Spades

Calculate your score. Ten points for each correct answer.

1) c, 2) c, 3) c, 4) a, 5) d, 6) b, 7) a, 8) a

Remember that learning poker is not easy!

Find which player you most resemble from "This Is What a Poker Hand Looks Like."

0-30 points: Lila Lackadaisical

Oh, dear... maybe poker isn't the game for you. I know you're trying, but, well, try harder.

40-60 points: Kyle Kewl

There's a saying, "Aim for the sky and you'll reach the ceiling. Aim for the ceiling and you'll stay on the floor." Take your goals seriously if you want to see results. As serious as you take your hair.

70-90 points: Alyssa Smart

Are you writing this book or am I? You're so good at poker you could be a teacher! Go easy on me, sister – you're a pro.

Quiz Level Four: Diamonds

Calculate your score. Ten points for each correct answer.

1) b, 2) b, 3) d, 4) c, 5) a, 6) a1, b4, c3, d2, 7) a, 8) a, b, c and d

Your results speak for themselves — unless your body does the talking? Let's try and get a read on you.

0-30 points: Fold

You gave poker a try, and, well, it wasn't for you. It doesn't take a secret agent to know that you're ready to fold. Toss those cards into the muck and let's move on.

40-60: Call

You're ready to play. I can see you're interested. Don't curb your enthusiasm, but do work on your timing. You're doing great — save for a few fidgety fingers!

60-80: Raise

Talk about girl power! You've got the look of a woman ready to take charge — no matter what cards life deals you. To paraphrase Sophia Loren, "beauty is 50 per cent what you got, and 50 per cent what people think you got."

Conclusion

The original manuscript for *A Girl's Guide to Poker* was a tutorial subtitled "Learn Poker in Under an Hour!" My how things changed.

Thank you for coming with me on this poker journey, and allowing me to kickstart your Texas Hold'em career. We need more women at the tables. We need more newcomers. We need more readers. *The fact that you're reading this reveals something very special about your personality.* It's an honor to be in your company.

Remember to do your homework. Learn the odds. Build a bankroll. Respect the game selection deal-breakers.

Also remember that it's OK to make mistakes.

We're not meant to play like computers. We're meant to play like people.

Good Luck,

Amanda

P.S. Thanks, Mom!

PRO TIP
Continue your poker journey
at amandasaces.com

♥✦ Amanda's Aces ♠♣

Hey there,

Check out Amanda's Aces – the official training website (amandasaces.com) of *A Girl's
Guide to Poker*.

Here you can play, practice, or (my favorite!)
shop.

Just make sure to have fun.

Your Friend on the Felt,

Amanda